UNIX
Quick Reference Guide

by Anatole Olczak

ASP, Inc.
PO Box 23837, San Jose California USA 95131
(800) 777-UNIX

UNIX QUICK REFERENCE GUIDE

ASP offers a full line of technical reference manuals, guides, and quick reference cards for UNIX, X Windows, C/C++, JavaScript, HTML, and other topics. They are specifically designed for the professional who needs easy-to-access reference information to increase productivity. Please call or email (**books@aspinc.com**) for more information.

TYPOGRAPHIC CONVENTIONS

Control characters are given as **Ctl** followed by the character in boldface. For example, **Ctl-d** specifies **Control-d** and is entered by pressing the **d** key while holding down the **Control** key. **Boldface** indicates items which must be typed exactly as given, *Italics* indicate items that are to be substituted, and brackets ([ ]) indicate optional items.

ISBN 0-935739-25-4

Introduction

This handbook is designed to be a reference and learning tool for the UNIX user. It is based on UNIX System V Release 4, but also contains some of the Solaris and BSD extensions. BSD-based commands are located in the **/usr/ucb** directory. A number of commands exist in both, so if **/usr/ucb** is specified in **PATH** before the standard directories, the BSD versions of the commands will be used instead. Some of these commands are:

apropos	**ln**	**rwho**
basename	**lpq**	**sccs**
biff	**lpr**	**script**
cc	**lprm**	**stty**
chown	**ls**	**sum**
clear	**man**	**tftp**
df	**mkstr**	**touch**
du	**more**	**tr**
echo	**netstat**	**tset/reset**
file	**page**	**users**
finger	**pagesize**	**vacation**
fmt	**printenv**	**w**
fold	**ps**	**wc**
from	**quota**	**whatis**
ftp	**rdist**	**whereis**
groups	**reset**	**whoami**
head	**rlogin**	**whois**
ld	**ruptime**	**xstr**

Each command section lists the title, and the invocation syntax. When applicable, options, variables, files, and related commands are also listed. Most of the commands also contain one or more examples. The invocation syntax uses a "**#**" system prompt to indicate that the commands can only be executed as super-user. The "**$**" system prompt is used to indicate that the command can be executed by anyone.

Each command also lists the group or type of command that it belongs to and includes the following:

BSD	BSD Extensions
FILE	File Management Commands
MISC	Miscellaneous Commands
PRINT	Print-related Commands
PROG	Programming Utilities
SCCS	SCCS Commands
SYSTEM	System Commands

Please send us any comments or suggestions. We will send you the next edition if we use any of your comments or suggestions.

admin - Create and Administer SCCS Files (SCCS)

$ admin [*options*] *files*

Description:

The **admin** command creates new and modifies existing SCCS files.

Options:

–a*name*	add *name* to list of users who can update the SCCS file with **delta**. The name can be a single or multiple login names, a group ID, or nothing. A group ID specifies all group members, and no ID specifies anyone. If *name* is preceded by **!**, update permission is denied. Multiple **–a** options can be given.
–d[*flag*]	remove *flag* from the SCCS file (see **–f** for flag value). Multiple **–d** options can be given.
–e*name*	remove *name* from list of users who can update the file with **delta**; *name* can be single or multiple login names, or a group ID. A group ID specifies all group members. Multiple **–e** options can be given.
–f[*flag*]	add *flag* to the SCCS file. Multiple **–f** options can be given on a single command line. Valid flags are:

b	allow branch delta creation (w/**–b**)
c*n*	set max release to *n* (default **9999**)
d*n*	set default delta for **get** to *n*
f*n*	set lowest release to *n* (default **1**)
i[*string*]	interpret **No id keywords** message from **get** or **delta** as fatal error. Keywords must match *string* if given. *string* must contain a keyword and no newlines;
j	allow multiple updates via **get** on same delta
l*list*	lock list of releases against updates by **get –e**; list can contain single, multiple comma-separated release numbers, or **a** for all.
m*string*	replace **%M%** keywords with *string* (default name of file without **s.** prefix)
n	create null deltas if skipping releases
q*string*	replace **%Q%** keywords with *string*
t*string*	replace **%Y%** keywords with *string*
v	make **delta** prompt for an MR number
v *prog*	use MR checking program *prog*

–h	verify structure and checksum of SCCS file
–i	create new SCCS file using text from **stdin**
–i*ifile*	create SCCS new file using text from *ifile*
–m	prompt for the MR numbers
–m*mrlist*	add MR numbers from *mrlist*
–n	create a new SCCS file (empty if no **–i**)
–r*rel*	use release *rel* for delta (only with **–i**; default **1.1**)
–t	remove descriptive text from existing file (with **–i** and **–n**)
–t *tfile*	replace descriptive text of existing file with text from *tfile*. If creating a new file, then *tfile* must be given.
–y[*text*]	insert *text* into comment line of file. If *text* not given, the default comment line "**date and time created** *yy/mm/dd hh:mm:ss* **by** *login*" is used. (only with **–i, –n**)
–z	recompute the checksum (see **–h**)

files	file names beginning with **s.**, –, or directory names. If *files* is a directory, then all files in directory beginning with **s.** are processed. If *files* is –, read file names from stdin.

Examples:

\# Create new **s.file** using **file**; allow branch deltas

$ admin –ifile –n s.file –fb

\# Add **jon** to list of users who can update**s.file**

$ admin –ajon s.file

\# Lock **s.file** against updating with **get –e** and **delta**

$ admin –fla s.file

apropos - Find Commands by Keyboard Lookup (BSD)

$ **/usr/ucb/apropos** *keywords*

Description:

The **apropos** command lists manual sections that contain the *keywords* in their titles.

ar - Archive and Library Maintainer (PROG)

$ ar [**–V**] *option* [*keys*] [*pos*] *archive* [*files*]

Description:

The **ar** command manipulates groups of files combined in a single archive file. One option, except **–V**, followed by one or more keys can be given. Options can be preceded with a dash.

Options:

d	delete *files* from *archive*
m	move *files* to end of *archive*. If **a**, **b** or **i** are given, a *pos* argument must be given.
	a — put new files after *pos*
	b — put new files before *pos*
	i — put new files before *pos*
p	display *files* in *archive*
q	append *files* to end of *archive* without checking
r[abiu]	replace *files* in *archive*. If **a**, **b** or **i** are given, a *pos* argument must be given. If **u** is given, only older archive files are updated. (see **m**)
t	display table of contents for *files* in *archive*. If no *files* given, display table of contents for entire archive.
x	extract *files* from *archive*. If no *files* are given, all files are extracted from archive.
–V	display version information

Keys:

c	suppress default creation diagnostic message
l	use current directory for temporary files (obsolete)
s	force regeneration of archive symbol table
v	provide verbose diagnostic messages when creating *archive*. If used with **–t**, a long listing displayed. If used with **–x**, each file is preceded with a name.
pos	name of file in archive used to specify a position

Examples:

List the files in the archive **file.a**

$ ar tv file.a

Update **hello.o** in the archive **file.a**

$ ar ru file.a hello.o

as - Common Assembler (PROG)

$ as [*options*] *file*

Description:

The **as** command assembles *file*according to *options*.

Options:

–m	run **m4** preprocessor on assembler input
–n	disable long/short address optimization (default enabled)
–o*file*	put assembler output in *file* (default *file*.**o**)
–On	suppress tool id information (default)
–Oy	put tool id information in output
–R	remove input file after completion
–T	accept obsolete assembler directives
–V	display assembler version number on **stderr**
–Y [**m**[**d**]], *dir*	get **m4** (**m**) and/or predefined (**d**) macro files from *dir*

at/batch - Execute Commands at a Later Time (SYSTEM)

$ at [**–f** *script*] [**–m**] *time* [*date*] [**+***n*]

$ at –l [*jobs*]

$ at –r *jobs*

$ batch

Description:

The **at** command executes commands read from **stdin** at *time*. The **batch** command executes commands read from **stdin** when system load level permits. Output is mailed to invoker, unless redirected.

Options:

–f*file*	read commands from *file*
–l	display all jobs scheduled for invoker
–l *jobs*	display information about *jobs*
–m	send mail to user after completion
–r *jobs*	remove *jobs* from queue
[**am**|**pm**]*time*[**zulu**]	If **am** or **pm** is not appended to *time*, a 24-hour clock is used, **zulu** indicates GMT; **midnight**, **next**, **noon**, and **now** can also be used. Valid formats are: *h* , *hh*, *hhmm*, *hh*:*mm*
date	day name or month name followed by a day number and an optional comma and year number. The strings **today** and **tomorrow** can also be used. If no *date* is given, **today** is used if *time* is greater than the current time. **tomorrow** is used if *time* is less than the current time. If the month is less than the current month and no year is given, the next year is used. Day names can be abbreviated to 3 characters.
+*n*	number *n* followed by **days**, **hours**, **minutes months**, **weeks**, or **years** (singular forms are also accepted)

Examples:

\# Execute **who –a** at **3:00** tomorrow

$ at 3:00 tomorrow
who –a
^D

\# Execute **xferjob** when the system load level permits

$ xferjob | batch

\# List the **at/batch** jobs scheduled to be run for you

$ at –l

atq - Display Queued at Jobs (SYSTEM)

$ atq [*options*]
 # atq [*options*] *users*

Description

The **atq** command displays queued **at** jobs for the invoker. The super-user can display all **at** jobs, or just those for *users*.

Options:

–c	display queued jobs in creation order
–n	display total number of jobs in queue

Examples:

\# Display total number of jobs in queue

$ atq –n

atrm - Remove at Jobs (SYSTEM)

$ atrm [*options*] *jobs*
 # atrm [*options*] *jobs*

Description:

The **atrm** command removes **at** jobs.

Options:

–a	remove all jobs. If invoked by super-user, all jobs removed.
–f	suppress removal information
–i	prompt to verify before removal
jobs	user or job number

Examples:

\# Prompt to remove all jobs

$ atrm –ai

awk - Pattern Scanning and Processing Language (PROG)

$ awk [*options*] ['*program*'] [*params*] [*files*]

Description:

The **awk** command performs actions for lines in *files* that match *patterns* given in *program*.

Options:

–f*file*	get patterns from *file* instead of *program*
–F*c*	separate fields with character *c* (default whitespace)
params	parameters have the format *var=expr*
files	read **stdin** if *files* is – or no *files* are specified

Program Structure:

Each pattern in *program* can be associated with an action to perform if an input line matches the pattern. The format is:

pattern { *action* }

pattern	one or more arithmetic, regular, or string expressions separated by ",". A missing pattern always matches. The special patterns **BEGIN** and **END** specify an action to be performed before or after the input is read.
action	one or more *statements*. If { *action* } is missing, the current input line is displayed. Statements can be:
break	exit from **for** or **while** loop
continue	execute next **for** or **while** loop
exit	skip remaining input
for (*expr1; condition; expr2*) *statement*	
	execute *statement* while *condition* is true (loop is usually initialized with *expr1* and incremented with *expr2*)
if (*condition*) *statement1* [**else** *statement2*]	
	execute *statement1* if *condition* is true, otherwise execute *statement2*
next	skip rest of input line
print [*expression-list*] [> *expr*]	
	display *expression-list*; output can be redirected to a file
printf *format* [,*expression-list*] [> *expr*]	
	display *expression-list* according to format (like C function **printf** format); output can be redirected to a file
while (*condition*) *statement*	
	execute *statement* while *condition* is true

*var=expr*set *var* to *expr* (see **Operators**)

Operators:

var=expr1	set *var* to *expr*
var+=expr	set *var* to *var* plus *expr*
var–=expr	set *var* to *var* minus *expr*
var=expr*	set *var* to *var* times *expr*
var/=expr	set *var* to *var* divided by *expr*
var%=expr	set *var* to *var* modulo *expr*
var++	increment *var*
var—	decrement *var*
+, –, *, /, %	plus, minus, multiply, divide, remainder
<, < =	less than, less than or equal to
==, !=	equal to, not equal to
>, >=	greater than, greater than or equal to
exp1||*exp2*	*exp1* OR *exp2*
exp1&&*exp2*	*exp1* AND *exp2*
!*exp*	NOT *exp*
~*string*	contains *string*
!~*string*	does not contain *string*

Variables:

FILENAME	contains input file currently being read
FS	contains input field separator (default blank, tab)
NF	contains number of fields in current record
NR	contains current record number
OFMT	contains output format for numbers (default **%g**)
OFS	contains output field separator (default blank)
$RS	contains output record separator (default newline)
RS	contains input record separator (default newline)
$0	contains entire current input record
$*n*	contains *nth* input field of current record

Functions:

exp(*expr***)**	exponential of *expr*
getline()	read next input record
index(*s1,s2***)**	return position of string *s1* in string *s2*
int(*expr***)**	return integer value of *expr*
length(*s***)**	return length of string *s*
log(*expr***)**	return natural logarithm of *expr*
split(*s1,a***)**	split *s1* into *a*[**1**]-*a*[*n*] using **$FC**
split(*s1,a,c***)**	split *s1* into *a*[**1**]-*a*[*n*] using *c*
sprintf(*fmt,expr***)**	format *expr* according to **printf** format *fmt*
substr(*s,x***)**	return suffix of string *s* starting at *x*
substr(*s,x,n***)**	return *n*-character substring of *s* starting at *x*

Examples:

\# Display the first and third fields of **file**

$ awk '{print $1, $3}' file

\# Display field 2 of **file** if field 5 or field 6 greater than 7

$ awk '{if ("$5" > "7" || "$6" > "7") print $2}' file

\# Count numbers in field 3 of **file1**, then display the total

$ awk '{X+=$3} END {print "Total=",X}' file1

banner - Display Banner (**MISC**)

$ banner *strings*

Description:

The **banner** command displays *strings* in large letters on **stdout**. The *strings* arguments can contain up to ten characters each.

Examples:

\# Display **HELLO** in large letters

$ banner "HELLO"

basename - Display Parts of Pathnames (**MISC, BSD**)

$ basename *pathname* [*suffix*]

$ /usr/ucb/basename *pathname* [*suffix*]

Description:

The **basename** command displays part of *pathname* without the prefix ending in **/** and the *suffix*.

Examples:

\# Display last part of **/usr/spool/text.o** without the suffix **.o**

$ basename /usr/spool/test.o .o

batch - (see **at**)

bc - Arbitrary-Precision Arithmetic Language (**MISC**)

$ bc [**–c**] [**–l**] [*files*]

Description:

The **bc** command is an interactive arithmetic language processor.

Options:

–c	compile only; send the output to **stdout**
–l	use the arbitrary precision math library
files	read **stdin** after all *files*

bdiff - Compare Two Large Files (**FILE**)

$ bdiff *file1 file2* [*n*] [**–s**]

Description:

The **bdiff** command compares two files and displays lines that are different. It is used for files that are too large for **diff**.

Options:

–s	suppress **bdiff** diagnostic messages
n	split into *n*-line segments (default **3500**)
files	read **stdin** if *file1* or *file2* is **–**

Examples:

\# Compare two versions of the **/etc/hosts** file

$ bdiff /etc/hosts /etc/hosts.org

bfs - Scan Large Files (**FILE**)

$ bfs [**–**] *file*

Description:

The **bfs** command is a read-only **ed**-like utility. It is used to process larger files that **ed** cannot handle as efficiently.

Options:

–	do not display the file size

biff - Enable/Disable Mail Notification (**BSD**)

$ **/usr/ucb/biff** [*options*]

Description:

The **biff** command controls mail notification.

Options:

n	do not notify user when mail arrives
y	display header and first lines when mail arrives

cal - Display Calendar (**MISC**)

$ cal [[*month*] [*year*]]

$ cal

Description:

The **cal** command displays a calendar for *year*. If *month* is given, display a calendar for just that month, otherwise display a calendar for current month only.

Options:

month	number between **1** and **12**
year	number between **1** and **9999**

calendar - Reminder Service (MISC)

$ calendar [–]

Description:

The **calendar** command displays entries from the **calendar** file in the current directory that match today's or tomorrow's date. Each **calendar** entry contains a month/day pair.

Options:

–	execute **calendar** for all users with calendar files in their home directories and mail entries for today and tomorrow

cancel - Cancel Print Request (PRINT)

$ cancel [*print-request-ids*| *printer*]

 # cancel –u *user* [*printer*]

Description:

The **cancel** command cancels print requests printing on *printer*. If no print request id given, cancel current request. If no *printer* given, use default printer. The super-user can cancel print requests for any users.

Options:

–u *user*	cancel print requests for user (super-user only)

Examples:

Cancel the print request associated with id **53**

$ cancel 53

Cancel all requests for user **fred**

 # cancel –u fred

cat - Display Files (FILE)

$ cat [*options*] *files*

Description:

The **cat** command displays *files* according to given options.

Options:

–e	display **$** at the end of each line (only with **–v**)
–s	suppress error messages about non-existent files
–t	display tab characters as **^I**'s, formfeeds as **^L**'s
–u	do not buffer the output
–v	make non-printable characters visible. ASCII control characters (octal **000–037**) are displayed as ^*n*, where *n* is the ASCII character in the octal range 100–137.
files	read **stdin** if *files* is – or no *files* specified

Examples:

Append the contents of **file1** to **file2**

$ cat file1 >> file2

Display binary file **a.out**; pipe output through **more**

$ cat –v a.out | more

cb - C Program Beautifier (PROG)

$ cb [–s] [–j] [–l *n*] [*files*]

Description:

The **cb** command formats C source code from *files*.

Options:

–j	reassemble split lines
–l *n*	split lines longer than *n* characters
–s	use Kernighan and Ritchie format
files	read **stdin** if no *files* specified

Examples:

Format **hello.c** and split lines longer than 65 characters

$ cb –l 65 hello.c

cc - C Compiler (PROG)

$ cc [*options*] *files*

$ /usr/ucb/cc [*options*] *files*

Description:

The **cc** command compiles C source code in *files*. File names ending in **.c** are treated as C source programs. File names ending in **.s** are treated as assembly source programs. File names ending in **.i** are treated as preprocessed C source programs.

Options:

–A*name*[(*token*)]	associate *name* with *token* as if by **#assert**
–A –	do not use any predefined macros and assertions
–B*file*	find substitute compiler passes in *file* with suffix **cpp**, **ccom**, or **c2**. Use **/usr/c** if no *file* given (**BSD**)
–B dynamic	link with **lib***x***.so** first (see **–l***x* option)
–B static	link with **lib***x***.a** first (see **–l***x* option)
–c	suppress link-edit phase; produce **.o** files
–C	do not delete comments
–dn	use static linking
–dy	use dynamic linking (default)
–D*var*	define *var* as 1
–D*var*=*val*	define *var* as *val*
–E	send only preprocessor output to **stdout**
–f	do not convert expressions with only floats (**BSD**)
–g	generate **sdb** debugger information
–g	produce symbol table information for **dbx** (**BSD**)
–go	produce symbol table information for **sdb** (**BSD**)
–G	produce shared object instead of dynamic link
–H	display pathname of each **#include** file on **stderr**
–I*dir*	search for **#include** files in *dir* first
–J sfm	use assembly language math library **libsfm.sa**

–K[*mode*, *goal*, **PIC**, **miniabi**]

mode	**fpe** (software floating point emulation)
	mau (hardware math accelerator unit)
goal	**sd** (optimize for speed)
	sz (optimize for size)
PIC	generate position-independent code
miniabi	minimize dynamic linking

–l*x*	search library **lib***x***.a** (default **LIBDIR** or **LLIBDIR**)
–L*dir*	add *dir* to the library search list
–M	generate **Makefile** dependencies (**BSD**)
–o*file*	put output in *file* (default **a.out**)
–O	invoke object code optimizer
–p	set up an execution profile in **mon.out** (see **prof**)
–p[**g**]	set up execution profile for **prof** or **gprof** (**BSD**)
–P	send only preprocessor output to *file***.i**
–ql	invoke basic block analyser
–qp	set up object files for profiling (same as **–p**)
–Qn	suppress tool id information
–Qy	put tool id information in output (default)
–R	make initialized variables shared and read-only
–S	put assembler language output in *file***.s**
–t [*pass*]	specify which compiler pass to use from **–B***file* (**BSD**) option. The *pass* can be:

p	preprocessor
0, 1	compiler; first or second pass
2	optimizer

–U*var*	remove the definition of *var*
–v	perform strict semantic checks
–V	display version information
–w	suppress warning messages

–W*tool*, *args*

set arguments for the given compiler *tool*:

p	preprocessor	**a**	assembler
0	compiler	**b**	basic block analyser
2	optimizer	**l**	link editor

–Xa	conform to ANSI standards, but warn about integral promotion rule changes
–Xc	conform to ANSI standards
–Xt	accept compatible pre-ANSI code, warn about differences

–Y *tool*, *pathname*

use *pathname* as location of program associated with *tool*:

p	preprocessor	**l**	link editor
0	compiler	**S**	startup directory
2	optimizer	**I**	search last for include files
a	assembler	**P**	replace search libraries
b	basic block analyser		

Examples:

Compile **hello.c** and send the output to **hello**

```
$ cc hello.c –o hello
```

Compile **file.c**, and look for **#include** files in **/tmp/include**

```
$ cc –DDEBUG –I/tmp/include file.c –o file
```

cd - Change Working Directory (FILE)

$ cd [*directory*]

Description:

The **cd** command changes the current working directory to *directory*. If *directory* is not given, **$HOME** is used. If *directory* is not an absolute pathname, **$CDPATH** is searched.

Variables:

CDPATH	contains a list of colon-separated directory names to search when relative pathnames are given

Examples:

Change the current working directory to **/usr/spool/news**

$ cd /usr/spool/news

Change directory to one level above

$ cd ..

cdc - Change Delta Commentary of an SCCS Delta (SCCS)

$ cdc –r*SID* [**–m**[*mrlist*]] [**–y**[*text*]] *files*

Description:

The **cdc** command changes the delta commentary for *SID* for each file given. The delta commentary is the MR and comment information that is usually given by the **delta** or **admin** commands. If *files* is a directory, then all files in directory that begin with **s.** are processed.

Options:

–m	prompt for the MR numbers
–m*mrlist*	add MR numbers from *mrlist* if **v** flag is set (see **admin**). If MR number is preceded by **!**, the MR number is deleted. If **v** flag is set, a non-zero exit status from MR validation program causes **cdc** to exit and no changes to be made. The *mrlist* contains MR numbers separated by blanks or tabs; **!** before an MR number specifies deletion.
–r*SID*	specify delta *SID*
–y	prompt for comment field
–y*text*	replace comment field with *text*
files	file names beginning with **s.**, **–**, or directory names. If *files* is a directory, then all files in the directory beginning with **s.** are processed. If *files* is **–**, read file names from **stdin**.

Examples:

Change the MR associated with delta **3.1** of **s.file**

$ cdc –r3.1 –m135 s.file

cflow - Generate C Flow Graph (PROG)

$ cflow [**–r**] [**–ix**] [**–i_**] [**–d***n*] *files*

Description:

The **cflow** command takes **C**, **yacc**, **lex**, assembler, and object files as input and builds an external reference graph. If the nesting level gets too deep, use the **–e** option with **pr** to compress tab characters.

Options:

–d*n*	set nesting depth to *n* for the flow graph
–i_	include names that begin with an underscore
–ix	include static and external data symbols
–r	list the callers of each function

Examples:

Generate a flow graph for **hello.c**; include function callers

$ cflow –r hello.c

chgrp - Change Group ID of Files (FILE)

$ chgrp [*options*] *group files*

Description:

The **chgrp** command changes the group ID of *files* to *group*. The set user and group ID bits are cleared if invoker is not the super-user. Only the owner or super-user can change the group ID.

Options:

–h	change group ID of symbolic link, not file
–R	recursively descend subdirectories and change group ID of all files encountered
group	decimal group ID or group name

Examples:

Change the group ID of **file** to **110**

$ chgrp 110 file

Change group ID of all files in **/usr/lib/news** to **news**

$ chgrp –R news /usr/lib/news

chkey - Encrypt a Key (MISC)

$ chkey

Description:

The **chkey** command prompts for a password to encrypt a new key.

chmod - Change Access Modes of Files (FILE)

$ chmod [*options*] *absolute-mode files*

$ chmod [*options*] *symbolic-mode files*

Description:

The **chmod** command changes permissions of *files* according to the given mode. Only the owner or superuser can change a mode. To enable the set-group-ID bit, the group execution bit must be set and the invokers group ID must be the same as the file's.

Options:

–R recursively descend subdirectories and change mode of all files encountered

absolute-mode

has the form: [xxxx] where x is the OR of the following modes and n can be **7** (read/write/execute), **6** (read/write), **5** (read/execute), **4** (read), **3** (write/execute), **2** (write), or **1** (execute):

4000	set user ID on execution
20#0	set group ID on execution if **#** is **1**, **3**, **5**, or **7**; enable mandatory locking if **#** is **0**, **2**, **4** or **6**.
1000	save the text image after execution
0n**00**	owner permission
00n**0**	group permission
000n	other permission

symbolic-mode

has the form: **[agou] [+–=] [rstwxl]** (multiple symbolic modes must be separated with commas)

a	user, group and other permission (default)
g	group permission
o	other permission
u	owner permission
+	add permission
–	remove permission
=	assign absolute permission
r	read permission
s	set-user-ID or group-ID (with **g** or **u**)
t	save text mode
w	write permission
x	execute permission
l	mandatory locking during access

Examples:

Make **file** readable/writable by owner, readable by all

$ chmod 644 file

Enable the set user ID for **file**

$ chmod u+s file

Enable mandatory locking for access

$ chmod +l file

chown - Change User-ID of Files (FILE, BSD)

$ chown [*options*] *user files*

$ /usr/ucb/chown [*options*] *user files*

Description:

The **chown** command changes the user-ID of *files* to *user*. The set user and group ID bits are cleared if the invoker is not the super-user. Only the owner or super-user can change the user-ID of a file.

Options:

–f	do not report errors (BSD)
–h	change user ID of symbolic link, not file
–R	recursively descend subdirectories and change user ID of all files encountered
user	decimal user-ID or user name

Examples:

Change the user-ID of **file** to **sadm**

$ chown sadm file

Change user ID of **/var/spool/news** and files to **news**

$ chown –R /var/spool/news

clear, cmp, cof2elf, col, comb

clear - Clear Terminal Screen (MISC)

$ clear

Description:

The **clear** command clears your terminal screen.

cmp - Compare Two Files (FILE)

$ cmp [*options*] *file1 file2*

Description:

The **cmp** command compares *file1* and *file2* and displays the differing byte and line numbers.

Options:

–l	display byte number and differing bytes for each difference
–s	do not display file differences (return exit codes)
file1	read standard input if *file1* is –

Examples:

\# Compare **group** and **group.old**

$ cmp group group.old

cof2elf - COFF to ELF Object File Translation (PROG)

$ cof2elf [*options*] *files*

Description:

The **cof2elf** command converts COFF files to ELF format.

Options:

–i	ignore translation errors
–q	suppress messages
–Qn	do not put id information in the output (default)
–Qy	put id information in the output
–s*dir*	save copy of input files in *dir*
–V	display version information on **stderr**

col - Filter Reverse Line-Feeds (FILE)

$ col [*options*]

Description:

The **col** command reads standard input and performs the line overlays for forward and reverse line feeds.

Options:

–b	use a non-backspacing output device
–f	enable forward half line-feed
–p	do not ignore unknown escape sequences
–x	do not convert whitespace to tabs

comb - Combine SCCS Deltas (SCCS)

$ comb [*options*] **s.***file* **. . .**

Description:

The **comb** command generates a shell script which, when run, reconstructs the specified SCCS files. The shell script is displayed on standard output. If no options are specified, only the leaf deltas and the minimal number of ancestors are preserved. The comment field for the combined delta is changed to "**This was COMBined**".

Options:

–c*list*	retain only deltas from *list*
–o	set **get –e** access to release of new delta
–p*delta*	discard deltas older than *delta*
–s	display amount of space saved in the reconstruction
files	file names beginning with **s.**, **–**, or directory names. If *files* is a directory, then all files in it beginning with **s.** are processed. If *files* is **–**, read file names from **stdin**.

Examples:

Create script that builds **s.file** w/o deltas older than **2.3**

$ comb –p2.3 s.file > comb.out

comm - Select/Reject Common Lines (FILE)

$ comm [*options*] *file1 file2*

Description:

The **comm** command reads *file1*, *file2* and displays lines only in *file1*, lines only in *file2*, and lines in both files.

Options:

–1	suppress lines unique from *file1*
–2	suppress lines unique from *file2*
–3	suppress lines in both *file1* and *file2*
files	read standard input if *file1* or *file2* is –

Examples:

Display only the lines common to both files

$ comm –12 file1 file2

Display only the lines unique to both files

$ comm –3 file1 file2

compress - Compress Files (FILE)

$ compress [*options*] [*files*]

Description:

The **compress** command compresses the specified files.

Options:

–b	use 16-bit code for compression encoding
–b *n*	use *n*-bit code for compression encoding (**9–16**)
–c	write to **stdout** instead of *file*.**Z**
–f	force compression of *files*
–v	display the percentage of reduction for each file
files	read **stdin** if no *files* given; put output in *file*.Z

Examples:

Compress all files in current directory, showing reduction

$ compress –v *

cp - Copy Files (FILE)

$ cp [*options*] *file1 file2*

$ cp [*options*] *files directory*

Description:

The **cp** command copies *file1* to *file2*, or *files* to *directory*. If *file2* is non-existent, the user-ID and group-ID are that of the invoker. Otherwise, the mode, user-ID, and group-ID stay the same. The sticky bit is cleared, unless the invoker is the super-user.

Options:

–i	prompt before overwriting existing target
–p	preserve modification times and permissions
–r	recursively copy files and subdirectories
—	specifies end of options (when arg begins with –)

Examples:

\# Copy all C source files to **/tmp**

$ cp –p *.c /tmp

\# Copy all files and directories in **tools** to **/usr/tbin**

$ cp –r tools /usr/tbin

cpio - Copy File Archives (FILE)

$ cpio –i [**bBcdfkmrsStuvV6**] [**–C** *n*] [**–E** *file*] [**–H** *hdr*] [**–I** *file* [**–M** *string*]] [**–R** *ID*][*patterns*]

$ cpio –o [**aABcLvV**] [**–C** *n*] [**–H** *hdr*] [**–O** *file* [**–M** *str*]]

$ cpio –p [**adlLmuvV**] [**–R** *ID*] *directory*

Description:

The **cpio** command copies file archives. File archives can also be copied to directories.

Options:

–i	copy in all files or those that match *patterns*
–o	copy files out
–p	copy files from **stdin** to *directory*

Modifiers:

–a	reset access times of input files after the copy
–A	append files to an archive given by **–O**
–b	reverse the byte order in each word (only with **–i**)
–B	block input/output to 5120 bytes per record (only with **–i**, or **–o** and character special device)
–c	write header information in ASCII format
–C *n*	block input/output to *n* bytes per record (default **512**; only with character special device)
–d	create directories if needed
–E *file*	*file* contains list of files to extract from archive
–f	copy all files except those in *patterns* (only w/**–i**)
–H *hdr*	read or write header information in *hdr* format: **crc**, **CRC** ASCII header with expanded device numbers

	odc ASCII header with small device numbers
	tar, **TAR** tar format
	ustar, **USTAR** IEEE/P1003 standard format
–I *file*	read input from *file*. If *file* is a character special device, then when the first medium has been read, replace the medium and type a carriage return to continue to the next medium. (only with **–i**)
–k	skip corrupted file headers and I/O errors
–l	link rather than copy files if possible (only w/**–p**)
–L	follow symbolic links
–m	retain the previous modification time
–M *str*	specify message to use when switching media; **%d** specifies to display sequence number of next media (only w/**–I** or **–O**)
–O *file*	send output to *file*. If *file* is a character special device, when first medium is full, replace medium and type a carriage return to continue to next medium. (only w/**–o**)
–r	interactively rename files; skip file on null input, and use original pathname if "**.**" is given
–R *ID*	reassign owner and group permissions for each file to user *ID* (super-user only)
–s	swap bytes within each halfword
–S	swap halfwords within each word
–t	display a table of contents of the input only
–u	copy unconditionally
–v	display a list of file names. If used with **–t**, the listing looks like output of **ls –l** command.
–V	display a dot for each file copied
–6	copy in a file with an older format (only with **–i**)
patterns	copy in files that match one or more patterns; regular expressions are recognized, and **!***pattern* specifies not to match the pattern. Patterns should be enclosed in double quotes, or the name of a file in the current directory will be used. (default *)

Examples:

Copy in all the files, except those in **/usr/local/bin**

$ cpio –icduf "/usr/local/bin/*" < /dev/rmt0

Copy out files from **/usr2** to tape

$ find /usr2 –mount –print | cpio –oBc > /dev/rst

Display a table of contents of the cpio file **files.cpio**

$ cpio –iBctv < files.cpio

Copy the files in the current directory to **/usr/tmp**

$ ls | cpio –pdu /usr/tmp

Extract files from **old.cpio** listed in **extract.list**

$ cpio –iBc –E extract.list < old.cpio

crontab - Manipulate **crontab** Files (SYSTEM)

$ crontab *file*
$ crontab *options*
 # crontab *options* [*user*]

Description:

The **crontab** command manipulates **crontab** files. Users can invoke **crontab** if their names are in **/usr/sbin/cron.d/cron.allow**. If it doesn't exist, then users are not allowed to execute **crontab** if their names are in **/usr/sbin/cron.d/cron.deny**. If neither file exists, only the super-user can invoke **crontab**. If **cron.allow** doesn't exist, and **cron.deny** exists but is empty, then anyone can execute **crontab**.

Options:

–e	edit current **crontab** file or create new one
–l	display the **crontab** file for the invoker
–r	remove the **crontab** file for the invoker
file	install *file* as the invokers **crontab** file. Read standard input if no *file* specified.
user	manipulate the **crontab** file for *user* (super-user only)

File Format:

The **crontab** file contains entries for each command to be run. The format for each entry is:

minute hour month-day month week-day command

where *minute* can be (**0–59**), *hour* can be (**0–23**), *month-day* can be (**1–31**), *month* can be (**1–12**), and *week-day* can be (**0–6**; **0**=Sunday). Each field can be * for all values, multiple values separated with commas, or values separated with a hyphen (to indicate a range). A % character in *command* field indicates a newline. The command is invoked by the invoker's shell, and the default environment has defined **HOME**, **LOGNAME**, **SHELL=/bin/sh**, and **PATH=:/bin:/usr/bin:/usr/lbin**. Standard output and error output are mailed to the invoker unless redirected.

Variables:

EDITOR contains pathname of editor to use with **–e**

Directories:

/var/spool/cron/crontabs
contains all the user **crontab** files

Files:

/usr/sbin/cron.d/cron.allow
contains the list of users allowed to use **cron**

/usr/sbin/cron.d/cron.deny
contains the list of users not allowed to use **cron**

Examples:

\# List crontab entries; put output in **cron.out**

$ crontab –l > out

\# Install **file.cron** as crontab file

$ crontab file.cron

\# Edit the crontab file

$ crontab –e

crypt - Encrypt/Decrypt Text (**MISC**)

$ crypt [*key*]
$ crypt [**–k**]

Description:

The **crypt** command encrypts or decrypts text read from standard input according to *key* and displays the encryption or decryption on standard output. If no *key* is given, the invoker is prompted for one.

Options:

–k	use key from **CRYPTKEY**

Variables:

CRYPTKEY
contains the encryption key for use with **–k**

cscope – Interactively Examine C Program (**PROG**)

$ cscope [*options*] *files*

Description:

The **cscope** program interactively examines C source files.

Options:

The **–I**, **–p**, **–T** options can also be given in **cscope.files**.

–b	build cross-reference only
–c	do not compress data
–C	ignore case when searching
–d	do not update the cross-reference
–e	suppress **^e** command prompt between files
–f *file*	use file as cross-reference file (default **cscope.out**)
–i *file*	get list of filenames from *file* (default command line or **cscope.files**)
–I *dir*	search *dir* for **#include** files (default **/usr/include**)
–l	use line-oriented interface
–L	do a single search when used with *–n*
–p *n*	display last *n* components of path (default **1**)
–P *path*	prepend *path* to relative pathnames (only with **–d**)
–s *dir*	look in *dir* for additional source files
–T	use only first eight characters to match against C symbols
–u	unconditionally build cross-reference
–U	do not check file time stampts
–V	display version information

csh - C Shell (PROG, MISC)

$ csh [*options*] [*args*]

Description:

The **csh** command is a command language interpreter. It executes commands read from the terminal, and from a file.

Options:

–b	do not interpret next command-line arguments as options (set-user-ID scripts not executed w/o **–b**)
–c *file* [*args*]	read commands from *file*; put *args* in **argv**
–e	exit if a command fails
–f	enable fast start; do not read **.cshrc** or **.login** files
–i	execute in interactive mode
–n	read commands without executing them
–s	read commands from standard input
–t	exit after reading and executing one command
–v	display input lines as they are read
–V	same as **–v**, except enable before reading **.cshrc** file
–x	display commands and arguments as executed
–X	same as **–x**, except enable before reading **.cshrc**

Command Execution Format:

cmd1; *cmd2*	execute *cmd1* followed by *cmd2*
cmd &	execute *cmd* asynchronously in the background
cmd1| *cmd2*	pass **stdout** of *cmd1* to **stdin** of *cmd2*
cmd1 |& *cmd2*	pass **stdout** and **stderr** of *cmd1* **stdin** of *cmd2*
cmd1 && *cmd2*	execute *cmd2* if *cmd1* returns successful exit status
cmd1 || *cmd2*	execute *cmd2* if *cmd1* returns unsuccessful exit status
cmd \	continue command onto the next line
(*cmd*)	execute command in the current shell

I/O Redirection Operators:

<*file*	redirect standard input from *file*
>*file*	redirect standard output to *file*. Create *file* if non-existent, else overwrite. If **noclobber** set, file must not exist, or an error will occur.
> !*file*	same as > *file*, except do not check if *file* exists
>&*file*	same as > *file*, except also redirect standard error
>& !*file*	same as > *file*, except redirect standard error and do not check if *file* exists
>>*file*	append standard output to *file*. Create *file* if non-existent, else overwrite. If **noclobber** set, file must not exist, or an error will occur.
>> !*file*	same as >> *file*, except do not check if *file* exists
>> &*file*	same as >> *file*, except also redirect standard error
>> & !*file*	same as >> *file*, except redirect standard error and do not check if *file* exists
<<*arg*	read from standard input until a line that is identical with *arg* or EOF is read

Alias Commands:

alias	display a list of alias names and their values
alias *name*	display the alias value for *name*
alias *name value*	
	create an alias *name* and set it to *value* (*value* may contain escaped history substitution syntax)

History Substitution:

Format: *event:word:modifiers*

event previous command from history file:

!*n*	command *n*
!–*n*	*nth* last command
!*string*	command that begins with *string*
!?*string*	command that contains *string*
!!	previous command
!{...}	separate substitution from adjacent characters
^*x*^*y*	substitute *x* for *y* on previous command line

word individual word from previous command (":" can be omitted if word begins with ^, $, *, –, or %).

#	entire command line
0	first word
n	*nth* argument
^	first argument
$	last argument
%	word matched by last ?*string* search
x–*y*	range of words from *x* to *y*
–*y*	range of words from first to *y*
*	all arguments (no match if only one word)
x–	range of words *x* to second to last arg

modifier controls command/word selection (multiple modifiers must be separated with a "**:**" character). If prefixed with **g**, then the modification is applied to all arguments.

e	return filename suffix of first argument
h	return root pathname part of first arg
p	display new command, but do not execute
q	quote substituted words to prevent further substitution
r	return filename prefix of first argument
s/*x*/*y*	substitute first occurrence of *x* for *y*
t	return tail pathname part of first arg
x	same as **q**, except quote words individually
&	repeat previous substitution

Filename Substitution:

?	match any single character
*	match zero or more characters
[abc]	match any characters between the brackets
[x–z]	match any character or characters in range **x** to **z**
[a–ce–g]	match any characters in the range **a** to **c**, **e** to **g**
{*s1*, *s2*, ...}	match any string in the given set
~	substitute the home directory of the invoker
~*user*	substitute the home directory of *user*

Job Control Commands:

bg [%*n*] put current or stopped job *n* in the background
fg [%*n*] move current or background job *n* into foreground
jobs display the status of all jobs
jobs –l display status of all jobs along with process ids
kill [–*signal*] [%*n* | PID]
send *signal* to job *n*, current job, or specified process-ID (default **TERM**)
kill –l list all valid signal names
notify [%*n*] notify user when status of current job or job *n* changes
stop [%*n*] stop current or specified job *n*
stty [–]**tostop**
allow/prevent background jobs from generating output
suspend suspend execution of the current shell
wait wait for all background jobs to complete
Ctl-z stop the current job

Job Name Format:

%, %%, %+ current job
%n job *n*
%– previous job
%string job whose name begins with *string*
%?string job that matches part or all of *string*

Quoting:

'...' remove special meaning of enclosed characters except '
"..." remove special meaning of enclosed characters except $, ', !, and \
c remove the special meaning of character *c*
\``cmd`\` replace with the standard output of *command*

Variable Assignment Format:

set *variable* set *variable* to null
set *variable=value*
set *variable* to *value*
set *variable*=(*value1 value2 . . . valuen*)
set *variable* to *value1* through *valuen*
set *variable*[*n*]=*value*
set *variable* element *n* to *value*
set *variable*[*n*]=(*value1 value2 . . . valuen*)
set *variable* element *n* to *value1* through *valuen*
unset *variable*
remove the definition of *variable*
@ *variable=expression*
set *variable* to numerical value of *expression*
@ *variable*[*n*]=*expression*
set *variable* element *n* to numerical value of *expression*

Variable Expansion Format:

Variable expansion can also be modified by appending a history substitution modifier (**:e**, **:gh**, **:gr**, **:gt**, **:h**, **:q**, **:r**, **:t**, or **:x**) to variable name. If braces are used, the modify operator must also be enclosed.

$variable, ${*variable*}
value of *variable*

$variable[n], *${variable[n]}*
  value of word *n* in *variable*

$variable[n–m]}*, *${variable[n–m]}
  values of words *n* through *m* in *variable*

$variable[–m], *${variable[–m]}*
  values of words 1 through *m* in *variable*

$#variable, *${#variable}*, *$variable[n–]*, *${variable[n–]}*
  number of words in *variable*

$0 name of file from which command input is being read

$n, *${n}* current shell argument *n* (same as $**argv**[*n*])

$* all current shell arguments (same as $**argv**[*])

These may not be used with the history substitution modifiers:

$?variable, *${?variable}*
  return string **1** if variable is set, else return **0**

$?0 return string **1** if current input file known, else return **0**

$$ process ID of the current shell

$< substitute a line from standard input

Environment Variables:

The C shell copies value of environment variables **HOME** into **home**, **PATH** into **path**, **TERM** into **term**, and **USER** into **user**, and copies each back whenever the shell variables are reset.

Environment Variable Assignment Format:

setenv *var* set environment variable *var* to null

setenv *var value*
  set environment variable *var* to *value*

unsetenv *variable*
  remove the definition of environment *variable*

Environment and Predefined Shell Variables:

argv number of arguments to the shell ($**1**, $**2**, . . .)

cdpath directory search path for **cd**, **chdir**, and **popd** when not given a full pathname or subdirectory

cwd full pathname of the current directory

echo display commands and arguments before execution

fignore filename suffixes to ignore during filename completion

filec enable filename completion. When typed at end of a command line, **Ctl-d** displays a list of all filenames that begin with the preceding string, and **Esc** replaces the preceding string with the longest extension.

hardpaths if set, links are resolved in the directory stack

histchars one or two character string; first character replaces **!**, second character replaces ^ in history substitutions

history number of previous commands accessible by the current shell (default only most recent command)

home pathname of home directory

ignoreeof if set, ignore **EOF** (**Ctl-d**) from terminal

mail list of files to check for mail. Number can be given before filename to specify mail checking interval.

nobeep suppress bell during command completion

noclobber if set, > redirections can only be made to new files, and >> redirections can only be made to existing files

noglob	if set, disable filename substitution
nonomatch	if set, no error is returned on non-matching filename substitution
notify	if set, user is immediately notified of completed jobs
path	list of pathnames to search for commands
prompt	string which is displayed before each command is read. A **!** is replaced with current command number (default *hostname%*, or *hostname#* for super-user).
savehist	number of command entries to save in **~/.history** between login sessions
shell	pathname of current shell
status	return status of last command
time	control timing of commands. Can have one or two values, where first value specifies reporting threshold in CPU seconds, and second value specifies which resource to report. Resources given by one or more:

%D	average Kbytes of unshared data space
%E	elapsed time
%F	number of page faults
%I	number of input block operations
%K	average Kbytes of unshared stack space
%M	maximum real memory used
%O	number of block output operations
%P	total CPU time
%S	CPU time used by kernel for user's process
%U	CPU time devoted to user process
%W	number of swaps
%X	average Kbytes of shared memory used

verbose	display each command after history substitution

Expressions:

Expressions can be given to the C Shell commands like @, **exit**, **if**, **set**, and **while**. The non-file operators are similar to those in the C programming language and have the same precedence.

File Operators:

–d *file*	true if *file* is a directory
–e *file*	true if *file* exists
–f *file*	true if *file* is a regular file
–o *file*	true if *file* owned by user
–r *file*	true if *file* is readable
–w *file*	true if *file* is writable
–x *file*	true if *file* is executable
–z *file*	true if *file* is zero length

Other Operators:

(...)	grouping (used to override precedence)
~	one's complement
!	logical negation
*, /, %	multiplication, division, modulo
+, –	addition, subtraction
<<, >>	bitwise shift left, bitwise shift right
<, >, <=, >=	less than, greater than, less than or equal to, greater than or equal to

==, !=, =~, !~
: equal to, not equal to, equal to pattern, not equal to pattern (used with strings)

&, ^, | bitwise AND, bitwise exclusive OR, bitwise OR
&& logical AND
|| logical OR
= assignment
++, -- increment, decrement
+=, -= add assign, subtract assign
*=, /=, %= multiply assign, divide assign, modulo assign

Control Commands:

foreach *var* (*word1 word2* **. . .** *wordn*)
commands
end Execute commands once for each *word* setting *var* to *word*. The **break** and **continue** commands can be used to terminate or continue the loop early.

goto *label* Continue execution after the line with *label*: (cannot be in a **while** of **for** loop).

if (*expr*) *command*
Execute a single command if *expr* returns true

if (*expr1*) **then**
commands1
else if (*expr2*) **then**
commands2
. . .
else *commands3*
endif Execute *commands1* if *expr1* returns true, otherwise execute *commands2* if *expr2* returns true. Execute *commands3* if *expr1* and *expr2* do not return true.

switch (*string*)
case *label*: *commands*
breaksw
case *label*: *commands*
breaksw
. . .
default: *commands*
breaksw
endsw Execute commands for the **case** statement whose *label* matches *string*. If no case statement matches *string*, then the commands associated with **default** are executed. The **breaksw** commands causes execution to resume after **endsw**.

while (*expr*)
commands
end Execute *commands* while *expr* is true. The **break** and **continue** commands can be used to terminate or continue the loop early.

Other Commands:

: null command; returns zero exit status

break exit from current enclosing **foreach**, or **while** loop

cd [*dir*], **chdir** [*dir*]
change directory to *dir*. If *dir* not specified, change directory to **$HOME**. If *dir* is a relative pathname not found in the current directory, **cdpath** is checked.

continue continue at start of next **foreach** or **while** loop

dirs display the current directory list

dirs –l display the current directory list in long format

echo *arguments*
display *arguments* terminated with a newline

echo –n *arguments*
display *arguments* without a terminating newline

eval *command*
evaluate *command* and execute the result

exec *command*
replace current process with *command*

exit exit from current program with value of **status**

exit (*expr*) exit from current program with value of *expr*

glob *arguments*
perform filename expansion on *arguments*

hashstat display statistics for hashing attempts

history display the command history list

history [**–hr**] *n*
display *n* previous commands from history list:

- **–h** display without command numbers
- **–r** display in reverse order

limit [**–h**] [*resource* [*limit*]]
set or display a resource limitation. If **–h** given (only by the super-user), then hard limits are used instead of the current limits. If no *limit* is given, then the current limit for *resource* is displayed. If no *resource* is given, all current limits are displayed. The *resource* can be one of:

- **cputime** maximum cpu seconds per process
- **filesize** largest single file allowed
- **datasize** maximum data size for the process
- **stacksize** maximum stack size for the process
- **coredumpsize**
maximum size of core dump

limit is a number with an optional scale factor:

- *n***h** *n* hours (**cputime**)
- *n***k** *n* kilobytes (all except **cputime**)
- *n***m** *n* megabytes (all except **cputime**), or *n* minutes (**cputime**)
- *mm:ss* minutes and seconds (**cputime**)

login terminate a login shell, invoke **login** and prompt for name

login *user* terminate a login shell and login as *user*

login –p same as **login**, except preserve current environment

logout terminate a login shell

nice [*priority*] [*command*]
: increment/decrement process priority for the current shell or *command*. The *priority* can be (default **4**):

+*n*	increment process priority value by *n*
–*n*	decrement process priority value by
n	(super-user only)

nohup ignore hangups (HUP) in C shell scripts

nohup *command*
: execute *command* with hangups (**HUP**) ignored

onintr terminate C shell scripts on interrupt

onintr – ignore all interrupts

onintr *label*
: execute **goto** *label* on interrupt

popd discard top entry from directory stack

popd +*n* discard *nth* entry from directory stack

pushd switch top two directory stack elements

pushd +*n* switch *nth* directory stack entry and **cd** to it

pushd *dir* move current directory to top of stack and **cd** to *dir*

rehash recompute hash table

repeat *n command*
: execute *command n* times

set display a list of variable names and their values

shift [*var*] shift components of *var* once to the left, discarding the first component. If no *var* specified, use **argv**.

source [**–h**] *file*
: read and execute commands from *file*. If **–h** specified, read commands, but do not execute.

time display a summary of time used by current shell

time *command*
: display a summary of time used by *command*

umask display current value of the file creation mask

umask *mask*
: set default file creation mask to octal *mask*

unhash disable use of internal hash table

unlimit [*resource*]
: remove limitations from all or specified *resource*

unlimit –h [*resource*]
: remove hard limits from all or the specified *resource* (super-user only)

Miscellaneous:

anything following **#** to end of current line is treated as a comment and ignored. If first character of a script file is *#*, a C shell is invoked. Otherwise a Bourne shell is invoked.

#!interpreter run script via *interpreter*

Files:

~/.cshrc read at beginning of execution by C shell

~/.history contains previously executed commands

~/.login read by login shell after **.cshrc** file

~/.logout read by login shell at logout

csplit - Split Files (FILE)

$ csplit [**–s**] [**–k**] [**–f** *pre*] *file arg1* [*arg2 . . . argn*]

Description:

The **csplit** command splits *file* into *n*+1 files according to *args*. The split files are named **xx00-xx***n*. First split file is from beginning up to *arg1*, second split file is from *arg1* up to *arg2*, and so on. The original file is not affected.

Options:

–f *prefix*	name output files *prefix00–prefixn* (default **xx00**–**xx***n*)
–k	leave the created files intact if an error occurs
–s	do not display character counts
file	read standard input if *file* is –

Arguments:

/rexp/	create file for current line up to regular expression */rexp/*; may be followed by **+***n* or **–***n* to indicate a relative position
%rexp%	do not create file for current line up to regular expression *%rexp%*; may be followed by a **+***n* or **–***n* to indicate a relative position
n	create file for current line up to line *n*
{*n*}	repeat the previous argument *n* times

Examples:

\# Split **file** into separate sections and use **section** as the file prefix

$ csplit –f section file '/^Section/'

\# Split **file** into 200-line sections named **part***nn*

$ csplit –f part file 200

ct - Call Terminal and Start Login Process (MISC)

$ ct [**–w***n*] [**–x***n*] [**–h**] [**–v**] [**–s***speed*] *telno*

Description:

The **ct** command is used to call a modem that is attached to a terminal and start a **getty** process. It will attempt to dial out on each line in the **/usr/lib/uucp/Devices** file until an available line is found. If none is found, **ct** will prompt the invoker to wait and for how long. It will then attempt to dial out again at one-minute intervals. When the remote terminal logs out, the invoker is prompted again to reconnect. Type **^D** to log out properly.

Options:

–h	do not hang up the current line
–s*speed*	set the baud rate to *n* (default **1200**)
–v	send diagnostics to standard error
–w*n*	wait for an available line up to *n* minutes
–x*n*	set debugging level to *n* (**0–9**); higher number for more debugging information
telno	If more than one *telno* is given, each will be dialed until an answer is received; *telno* can also contain = (wait for a secondary dial tone), and – (pause)

Files:

/etc/uucp/Devices

contains local device configuration information

Examples:

\# Dial out to **5103824545** and start a login-process

$ ct –s2400 5103824545

ctags - Create a Tags File (**PROG**)

$ ctags [*options*] *files*

Description:

The **ctags** command creates a tags file for **ex** from the given C, Fortran, lex, Pascal, or YACC source files.

Options:

–a	append to tags file
–B	use backward searching patterns (**?...?**)
–f*tfile*	put tag descriptions in *tfile* (default **tags**)
–F	use forward searching patterns (**/.../**) (default)
–t	create tags for **typedefs**
–u	update specified files in tags file
–v	display index for **vgrind** which contains the function name, file name, and page number
–w	suppress warning messages
–x	display index of object name, line number, file, text line

ctrace - C Program Debugger (**PROG**)

$ ctrace [*options*] [*file*]

Description:

The **ctrace** command is a C program debugger that is used to trace the execution of C programs. To trace a program, redirect the output of **ctrace** into a file, then compile that file with **cc**.

Options:

–A*name*[(*token*)]	associate *name* with *token* as if by **#assert**
–A –	do not use any predefined macros and assertions
–D*var*	define *var* as 1 (with **–P**)
–D*var*=*val*	define *var* as *val* (with **–P**)
–e	display variables in floating-point format
–f *funcs*	trace the specified functions only
–I*dir*	search for **#include** files in *dir* first (with **–P**)
–l *n*	check *n* consecutively executed statements for looping output (default **20**). If *n* is **0**, all loops are traced.
–o	display variables in octal format
–p'*string*'	change default trace function from **printf(** to *string*
–P	run the C preprocessor before tracing
–Qn	do not add id information to output (default)
–Qy	add id information to output
–r *file*	use *file* instead of **runtime.c** trace function package
–s	suppress redundant trace output
–t *n*	trace *n* variables per statement (default **10**, max **20**)
–u	display variables in unsigned format
–U*var*	remove the definition of *var*
–v *funcs*	do not trace the specified functions
–x	display variables in hexadecimal format
file	read standard input if no *file* is specified

Examples:

\# Trace the execution for **helloworld.c**

$ ctrace –s –P helloworld.c > tmphello.c
$ cc –o tmphello tmphello.c

cu - Call Another Unix System (MISC)

$ cu [*options*] *destination*

Description:

The **cu** command is used to call up another system or a terminal. It also provides file transfer capabilities.

Options:

–b*n*	set character size to *n* bits
–c*type*	use device that matches *type*
–d	display diagnostic trace messages
–e	set even parity for sending data
–h	set communication mode to half duplex
–l*line*	specify device pathname to use. If used with **–s**, devices file is searched to see if *line* is available at the given baud rate. If there is no match, the call is not made. If used without **–s**, the baud rate is taken from the devices file.
–n	prompt for the phone number to dial
–o	set odd parity
–s*speed*	set baud rate to *n* (default **Any** from the devices file)
–t	dial out to an ASCII terminal with auto answer
destination	can be phone number, system name, or LAN address. The telephone number can also contain these characters: = wait for a secondary dial tone – pause

Commands:

~%break, **~%b**	send a **BREAK** to the remote system
~%cd	change directory on the local system
~%debug	toggle the **–d** debugging option
~%divert	do not allow unsolicited diversions
~%l	display termio structure variable value for remote line
~%nostop, **~%ifc**	toggle between Xon/Xoff and no protocol
~%noostop, **~%ofc**	toggle output flow control setting
~%old	toggle between allowing/disallowing old style syntax for received diversions
~%put *file1* [*file2*]	copy local *file1* to remote *file2*. If no *file2* is given, use *file1* on the remote system.
~%t	display termio structure variable value for local terminal
~%take *file1* [*file2*]	copy remote *file1* to local *file2*. If no *file2* is given, use *file1* on the local system.
~!	escape to an interactive shell on the local system
~!*cmd*	execute *cmd* on local system (via **sh –c**)
~$*cmd*	execute *cmd* locally; send output to the remote system
~~*string*	send *~string* to remote system; interpret *string* on the intermediate system between local and remote systems
~.	close the connection

Files:

/etc/uucp/Devices
contains information about the UUCP devices

/etc/uucp/Systems
contains information about the UUCP systems

Examples:

\# Call up another system and use 2400 baud rate
$ cu –l /dev/term/tty002 4083457222

\# Call up a system named **freddy**
$ cu freddy

\# Call up directly-connected system
$ cu –l /dev/term/aty12

cut - Display File Fields (FILE)

$ cut –c*list* [*files*]
$ cut –f*list* [– *c*] [**–s**] [*files*]

Description:

The **cut** command displays fields from lines in *files* according to selection options. The fields can be of fixed or variable length.

Options:

–c *list*	display characters from character positions in *list*
–d *c*	set field delimiter to *c* (default tab)
–f *list*	display fields specified in *list*
–s	suppress lines with no delimiter characters
files	read standard input if *files* are –, or no *files* are specified
list	comma separated list of integer field numbers; integers separated with a – indicate a range

Examples:

\# Display the first seven characters of each line in **file1**
$ cut –c1–7 file1

\# Display the first and fifth fields of **/etc/passwd**
$ cut –f1,5 –d":" /etc/passwd

cxref - Generate C Program Cross-Reference (PROG)

$ cxref [*options*] *files*

Description:

The **cxref** command generates a cross-reference table for the specified C program source files.

Options:

–A*name*[(*token*)]	associate *name* with *token* as if by **#assert**
–A –	do not use any predefined macros and assertions
–c	display a combined cross-reference for all input files
–C	run only first pass and create **.crx** file
–d	disable printing declarations
–D*var*	define *var* as 1
–D*var=val*	define *var* as *val*

–F	display full pathname of referenced file names
–I*dir*	search for **#include** files in *dir* first
–l	do not display local variables
–L*n*	set number of columns in **LINE** to *n* (default **5**)
–o*file*	send output to *file*
–s	suppress diagnostic messages
–t	format the output for 80-column width
–U*var*	remove definition of *var*
–V	display version information
–w*n*	set max output width to *n* characters (default **80**)

–W NAME,FILE,FUNCTION,LINE
change default width of field (default **NAME**=15, **FILE**=13, **FUNCTION**=15, **LINE**=20)

Examples:

\# Generate cross reference for **helloworld.c**

$ cxref –I/usr/local/include helloworld.c

date - Display or Set the Date (MISC)

$ date [*options*] [*+format*]
 # date [*options*] [*date*]

Description:

The **date** command displays or sets the date according to *options*. Different languages can be specified (see below).

Options:

–a [–] *sss.fff*
slowly adjust time by *sss.fff* (*fff* is fractions of a second)

–u	display or set date in GMT
+format	display the date according to *format*

[*mmdd*]*HHMM*
mmddHHMM [*cc*] *yy*]
set date using the given format (super-user only)

Format:

%a	abbreviated weekday name (**Sun–Sat**)
%A	full weekday name (**Sunday–Saturday**)
%b	abbreviated month name (**Jan–Dec**)
%B	full month name (**January–December**)
%c	country specific date and time format
%d	day of month (**01–31**)
%D	date as *mm/dd/yy*
%e	day of month (**1–31**)
%h	abbreviated month (**Jan–Dec**)
%H	hour (**00–23**)
%I	hour (**01–12**)
%j	day of year (**001–366**)
%m	month of year (**01–12**)
%M	minute (**00–59**)
%n	insert a newline character
%p	meridien indicator (**AM, PM**)

%r	time with AM/PM notation
%R	time as **%H:%M:%S %p**
%S	second (**00–59**)
%t	insert a tab character
%T	time as *hh:mm:ss*
%U	year week number (**00–53** Sunday is first week day)
%w	day of week (**Sun=0**)
%W	year week number (**01–52** Monday is first week day)
%x	country-specific date format
%X	country-specific time format
%y	last 2 digits of year (**00–99**)
%Y	year as *ccyy*
%Z	timezone name

Variables:

LC_TIME	contains default date format string
LANG	contains language to use for translating

Examples:

Display the date as "Day name month/day/year"

$ date '+%A %m/%d/%Y'

Display the week number and day of year

$ date '+%w %j'

dc - Desk Calculator (MISC)

$ dc [*file*]

Description:

The **dc** command is an arbitrary precision math package. Input is taken from *file*, then standard input.

Options:

file	read standard input after *file*

Operations:

+ – / * % ^	operations performed on top two stack elements
n	numbers can be from **0–9**, preceded by "_" (for negative numbers), or can contain decimal points

dd - Convert and Copy File (FILE)

$ dd [*options*]

Description:

The **dd** command copies input to output according to the conversion options. The number of output blocks is displayed upon completion. Where *n* is given as a size, the number of bytes can be specified by using the prefixes (**b**, **k**, or **w**) or the multiplier (**x**).

Options:

bs=*n*	set input/output block size to *n* (overrides **ibs/obs**)
cbs=*n*	set the conversion buffer size to *n*

conv=	**ascii**	convert EBCDIC to ASCII
	ebcdic	convert ASCII to EBCDIC
	ibm	convert different ASCII to EBCDIC
	lcase	map upper to lower case
	noerror	ignore errors
	swab	swap byte pairs
	sync	pad every input block to **ibs**
	ucase	map lower to upper case
	unblock	convert to variable length records
	...,...	comma separated conversions
count=*n*	copy only *n* input blocks	
files=*n*	number of input files to copy (tape)	
ibs=*n*	set input block size to *n* bytes (default **512**)	
if=*file*	specify input file name (default standard input)	
iseek=*n*	seek *n* blocks from beginning of input before copying	
of=*file*	specify output file name (default standard output)	
obs=*n*	set output block size to *n* bytes (default **512**)	
oseek=*n*	seek *n* blocks from beginning of output before copying	
seek=*n*	seek *n* blocks from beginning before copying	
skip=*n*	skip *n* blocks before copying (tape)	
n [**k**,**b**,**w**]	*n* times 1024 (**k**), 512 (**b**), or 2 (**w**) bytes	
n **x** *n*	*n* times *n* bytes	

Examples:

Copy in the first 700 blocks from **/dev/rst0** into **/tmp/file**

$ dd if=/dev/rst0 count=700 of=/tmp/file

Copy in first cpio tape image

$ dd if=/dev/ctapen of=tape1.cpio bs=16k

delta - Make a Change to an SCCS File (SCCS)

$ delta [*options*] *files*

Description:

The **delta** command puts the changes made to a file retrieved by **get –e** into the specified SCCS file.

Options:

–g*list*	ignore deltas from *list*
–m	prompt for the MR numbers
–m*mrlist*	add MR numbers from *mrlist* if **v** flag is set (see **admin**). If **v** flag is set, non-zero exit status from validation program will cause **delta** to exit and no changes to be made.
–n	save the edited file
–p	display delta differences in **diff** format
–r*SID*	specify delta *SID*
–s	suppress diagnostic messages
–y	prompt for the comment field
–y*text*	replace the comment field with *text*
files	file names beginning with **s.**, –, or directory names. If *files* is a directory, then all files in directory beginning with **s.** are processed. If *files* is –, read file names from **stdin**.

Examples:

Prompt for comments and MR before applying delta

$ delta –m –y s.file

Display the delta differences for **s.file**

$ delta –p s.file

df - Display the Number of Free Disk Blocks (**FILE, BSD**)

$ df [*options*] [*names*]

$ /usr/ucb/df [*options*] [*names*]

Description:

The **df** command displays the number of free blocks and inodes in file systems, or directories. The *names* argument can be a pathname to a device special file, or mount point for a file system. If a directory is given, information is displayed about the file system that it resides on.

Options:

–b	display only number of kilobytes free
–e	display only the number of files free
–F*type*	specify file system type
–g	display entire **statvfs** structure
–i	display available and used inode count (BSD)
–k	display allocation in kilobytes
–l	display information about local file systems only
–n	display only file system type
–o *opts*	provide file system-type specific options
–t	display total as well as free blocks and inodes
–V	display the command line, but do not execute

Examples:

Display total free blocks and inodes for **/usr** file system

$ df –t /usr

Display free blocks and inodes for local file systems

$ df –l

Display a list of file system types

$ df –n

diff - Compare File Differences (**FILE**)

$ diff [**–bitw**] [**–c**|**–C** *n* |**–D** *str* |**–e** | **–f** | **–h** | **–n**] *file1 file2*

$ diff [**–bilrsStw**] [**–c** |**–e** |**–f** | **–h** | **–n**] *dir1 dir2*

Description:

The **diff** command compares two files and displays lines which need to be changed to make the files the same. The default output contains **ed**-like commands to convert *file1* into *file2*, followed by text lines prefixed with < for lines from *file1*, and > for lines from *file2*. When comparing directories, files with the same names are compared.

Options:

–b	ignore trailing blanks, other whitespace compare equal
–c	list differences with 3 lines of context. Each difference separated by line with *'s, lines removed from *file1* marked with ––, lines added to *file2* marked with +, and changed lines from both files marked with !.
–C *n*	list differences with *n* lines of context (see **–c**)
–D *string*	create merged version of *file1* and *file2* with C preprocessor commands, so that compilation with (without) *string* defined produces *file2* (*file1*)
–e	generate **ed** script with **a**, **c**, and **d** commands to produce *file2* from *file1*.
–f	generate non-**ed** script to produce *file1* from *file2*
–h	quickly compare files (not with **–e** or **–f**)
–i	ignore case of letters
–l	produce output in long format
–n	generate **ed** script and show count of changed lines
–r	execute **diff** recursively on common subdirectories
–s	report identical files that are found
–S *file*	start directory **diff** at *file*
–t	expand tab characters in output
–w	ignore spaces and tabs; treat strings of spaces/tabs as equal
files	read **stdin** if *file1* or *file2* is **–**

Examples:

Create listing with 3 lines of context; ignore case/blanks

$ diff –bt hello.c new-hello.c

diff3 - Compare Three Files (FILE)

$ diff3 [**–eExX3**] *file1 file2 file3*

Description:

The **diff3** command compares 3 files and shows the results.

Options:

–e	create script for unique lines between *file2* and *file3*
–E	same as **–e**, except include overlapping changes
–x	create script for unique lines between all three files
–X	same as **–x**, except include overlapping changes
–3	generate **ed** script for unique lines of *file3*

dircmp - Compare Directories (FILE)

$ dircmp [**–d**] [**–s**] [**–w***n*] *dir1 dir2*

Description:

The **dircmp** command compares the contents of the given directories and lists the files unique to both. If no options are given, a list of files common to both directories is generated that indicates whether the contents are the same.

Options:

–d	compare contents of common files in both directories and indicate differences in **diff** format
–s	suppress messages about identical files
–w*n*	set output width to *n* characters (default **72**)

Examples:

Compare files with same name in **/etc/lib** and **/usr/lib**

$ dircmp –d /etc/lib /usr/lib

diffmk - Mark File Differences (FILE)

$ /usr/ucb/diffmk *oldfile newfile markedfile*

Description:

The **/usr/ucb/diffmk** command compares *oldfile* to *newfile* and creates *markedfile* with **troff** change requests to show differences where "|" indicates changed lines and "*" indicates deleted lines.

dirname - Display Parts of Pathnames (MISC)

$ dirname *path*

Description:

The **dirname** command displays all but the last part of *path.*

Examples:

\# Display the root pathname of **/var/spool/uucppublic**

$ dirname /var/spool/uucppublic

dis - Disassemble Object Code (PROG)

$ dis [*options*] *files*

Description:

The **dis** command generates an assembly language listing for the specified object or object archive files.

Options:

–d *section*	disassemble section *section*; display data offset from beginning of section
–D *section*	disassemble *section*; display actual data address
–F *function*	disassemble *function* only
–l *x*	disassemble library **lib***x***.a**
–L	find source labels in symbol table (only with **–g**)
–o	display numbers in octal format (default hexadecimal)
–s	perform symbolic disassembly
–t *section*	disassemble section *section* as text
–V	display version information

Examples:

\# Display an assembly listing for **foo1** and **foo2** from **libh.a**

$ dis –F foo1 –F foo2 libh.a

disable - Disable Line Printers (PRINT)

$ disable [*options*] *printers*

Description:

The **disable** command stops *printers* from printing **lp** requests. The current print requests are also stopped.

Options:

–c	cancel current print requests
–r	use default reason for disablement
–r *string*	use *string* as reason for disablement
–W	wait for current **lp** request to complete

Examples:

Disable printer **lpd** for periodic maintenance

$ disable –r"down for maintenance" lpd

Cancel all print requests for printer **sys-alp**

$ disable –c sys-alp

download – Download PostScript Fonts (**MISC**)

$ download [*options*] [*files*]

Description:

The **download** command prepends resident fonts to *files*.

Options:

–f	force complete scan of each input file
–H *dir*	get fonts from *dir* (default **/usr/lib/lp/postscript**)
–p *ptr*	check **/etc/lp/printers/***ptr***/residentfonts** before downloading
–m *name*	use *name* as font map table
files	read standard input if no *files* are given, or if *files* is –

Examples:

Download the GillSans font from **/tmp/ps**

$ download –H /tmp/ps m gillsans file

dpost – troff Postprocessor for PostScript Printers (**PRINT**)

$ dpost [*options*] [*files*]

Description:

The **dpost** command translates troff **files** into PostScript and writes the result on standard output.

Options:

–c *n*	print *n* copies of each page (default **1**)
–e *n*	set text encoding level to *n* (**0**, **1**, or **2**)
–F *dir*	use *dir* as the font directory (default **/usr/lib/font**)
–H *dir*	use *dir* as host resident font directory
–L *file*	use *file* as prologue (default **/usr/lib/postscript/dpost.ps**)
–m *n*	scale each page by factor *n*
–n *n*	print *n* logical pages per page (default **1**)
–o *list*	print only page numbers from *list*: *n1* — page *n1* *n1*, *n2*, *n3* — pages *n1*, *n2*, and *n3* *n1–n2* — pages *n1* through *n2* *–n1* — beginning to page *n1* *n1–* — page *n1* to end
–O	disable PostScript picture inclusion
–pl	use landscape
–pp	use portrait mode
–T *dev*	use font files for device *dev* (default **post**)
–w *n*	set line width to *n* points (default **.3** points)
–x *n*	offset horizontal axis by *n* inches; positive *n* moves origin right (default **0**)
–y *n*	offset vertical axis by *n* inches; positive *n* moves origin up
files	read standard input if *files* is **–**, or no *files* given

Examples:

Print **file** in landscape mode

$ cat file | troff –mm –Tpost | dposts –pl

Print pages 1–5 of **file**

$ pic file | tbl | troff –mm –Tpost | dpost –o 1–5

du - Summarize Disk Usage (SYSTEM, BSD)

$ du [*options*] [*directories* | *files*]

$ /usr/ucb/du [*options*] [*directories* | *files*]

Description:

The **du** command displays number of blocks in directories or files. If no directories or files given, use current directory.

Options:

–a	generate an entry for each file (default dir's only)
–r	do not suppress warning messages
–s	display grand total summary only

Examples:

Display the total number of blocks used in **/usr2**

$ du –s /usr2

Display number of blocks for **.Z** files in current directory

$ du –as *.Z

echo - Display Arguments (MISC, BSD)

$ echo [**–n**] [*arguments*]

$ /usr/ucb/echo [**–n**] [*arguments*]

Description:

The **echo** command displays *arguments* on standard output. C-like escape conventions are also recognized.

Options:

–n	do not add newline to output

Special Arguments:

\b	backspace
\c	display line without newline
\f	form feed
\n	newline
\r	carriage return
\t	tab
\v	vertical tab
\0*n*	1, 2 or 3 digit octal value
****	backslash

Examples:

Display the arguments, one per line

$ echo "arg1\narg2\narg3\n"

Display prompt without ending newline and sound bell

$ echo "Enter command: \c \07"

Display variable length variable **RECORD** in a box

$ echo "   *\r* $RECORD"

ed/red - Text Editor (FILE)

$ ed [*options*] [*file*]

$ red [*options*] [*file*]

Description

The **ed** command is a line-oriented text editor, while **red** is the restricted version which only allows editing in the current directory.

Options:

–C	edit an encrypted file; prompt for a key to use
–p *string*	use *string* as the prompt string
–s	do not display the character counts
–x	edit an encrypted file; prompt for the key to use

Addresses:

n	*nth* line
.	current line
$	last line
'*x*	line marked with *x*
n1, *n2*	address *n1* to address *n2*
+*n*	*n* lines after the current line
–*n*	*n* lines before the current line
/RE/	next line matching the regular expression RE
?RE?	previous line matching the regular expression RE

Commands:

The command format is: *address command*. For some commands, the default address is listed in parentheses. The address (**.**) or (.,.) indicates that the default command with no address applies to the current line, (**$**) to the last line, and (**1,$**) to all lines.

(.)**a**	add text after addressed line; end with "**.**" alone on line
(.,.)**c**	change text for addressed lines; end with "**.**" alone on line
(.,.)**d**	delete text for the addressed lines
e *file*	edit *file*
e!*cmd*	read output of the given UNIX command into buffer
E *file*	edit *file*; do not display diagnostics
E!*cmd*	same as **e!***cmd*
f	display current file name
f *file*	set current file name to *file*
(1,$)g/RE/*cmds*	execute commands for lines matching regular expression RE in the addressed lines
(1,$)G/RE/*cmds*	same as **g/RE/** except execute interactively (**a**, **c**, **g**, **G**, **i**, **v**, **V** are not allowed)
h	explain last **?** message
H	set/unset diagnostic explanation mode
(.)**i**	insert text before addressed line; end with "**.**" alone on line
(.,.+1)**j**	join addressed lines
(.)**k***x*	mark addressed line *x*
(.,.)**l**	show displaying special characters in addressed lines

(.,.)**m***n*	move addressed lines after line *n*
(.,.)**n**	display addressed text with line numbers
(.,.)**p**	display addressed text lines
P	set/unset * prompt mode
q	quit editor
Q	quit without checking if changes have been made
($)**r**[*file*]	read in *file* after addressed line. If no *file* is specified, use remembered file name.
($)**r!***cmd*	read output of *cmd* after addressed line
(.,.)s/RE/*string*	substitute first occurrence of regular expression RE with *string*. If *string* is **&**, then it is replaced with string matching RE on current line.
(.,.)s/RE/*string*/**g**	substitute all occurrences of regular expression RE with *string*. If *string* is **&**, then it is replaced with string matching RE on current line.
(.,.)s/RE/*string*/*n*	substitute *n*th occurrence of regular expression RE1 with *string*. If *string* is **&**, it is replaced with string matching RE on current line.
(.,.)**t***n*	copy addressed lines after line *n*
u	undo last substitution
(1,$)**v**/RE/*cmds*	execute *cmds* for lines in addressed lines not matching regular expression RE
(1,$)**V**/RE/*cmds*	like **v**/RE/*cmds*, except execute interactively
X	edit encrypted file during **r**, **e** or **x**
(1,$)**w**[*file*]	write addressed lines to *file*
(1,$)**w!***cmd*	use addressed lines as **stdin** to the UNIX command
($)=	display line number
!*cmd*	execute UNIX command
(. +*n*)	display line *n*

Regular Expressions:

String:	Matches on:
c	any non-special character *c*
c	any character *c*
^	beginning of string
$	end of string
.	any character except newline
[*sss*]	any characters in the sequence *sss*
[^*sss*]	any characters not in the sequence *sss*
[*s*–*z*]	any characters from the range *s* to *z*
*RE**	zero or more successive occurrences of regular expression RE
RE+	one or more occurrences of regular expression RE
RE?	zero or one occurrence of the regular expression RE
(*RE*)	regular expression *RE* (grouped)
RE1RE2	regular expression*RE1* followed by *RE2*
RE1 | *RE2*	regular expression *RE1* or *RE2*

edit, egrep, enable

edit - Text Editor (**FILE**)

$ edit [**–r**] [**–x**] [**–C**] *files*

Description:

The **edit** command is used to edit *files*. It operates like **ex** with **novice**, **report**, **showmode** set to **on**, **magic** set to **off**.

Options:

–C	edit an encrypted file; prompt for a key
–r	retrieve last saved version
–x	edit an encrypted file; prompt for a key

egrep - Search Files for Patterns (**FILE**)

$ egrep [*options*] '*expression*' [*files*]

Description:

The **egrep** command displays lines in *files* that contain the given full regular expression pattern.

Options:

–b	precede each line with the block number
–c	display only count of matching lines
–e *–expr*	search for expression that begins with –
–f *file*	get expressions from *file*
–i	ignore case of letters during comparisons
–l	display only names of files with matching lines
–n	display output with line numbers
–v	display all lines, except those that match *pattern*
expression	full regular expressions (see **ed** for more info)
files	read standard input of no *files* are specified

Examples:

Display the number of lines in **file** that contain **new york**

$ egrep –c 'new york' file

Display lines in **file1** that begin with **a**, **b**, **c**, or **z**

$ egrep '^[a–c,z]' file1

Display lines in **file** that contain **The**; ignore case

$ egrep –i v 'The' file

Display lines in **file1** that contain four-character words

$ egrep '....' file1

enable - Enable Line Printers (**PRINT**)

$ enable *printers*

Description:

The **enable** command allows *printers* to print **lp** requests.

Examples:

Enable printer **sysprinter**

$ enable sysprinter

env - Set or Display Environment (MISC)

$ env [–] [*variable=value* **. . .**][*command*[*arguments*]]

$ env

Description:

The **env** command executes commands with *variables* set to *values*. If no arguments given, current variables and their values are displayed.

Options:

–	ignore inherited environment
variable=value	set *variable* to *value*

Examples:

Run **backup** script with **DIR** set to **/usr/tmp**

$ env DIR=/usr/tmp /etc/backup

ex - Text Editor (FILE)

$ ex [*options*] *files*

Description:

The **ex** command is used to edit *files*.

Options:

–c *cmd*	begin by executing command *cmd*
–C	edit encrypted file; prompt for a key to use
–L	list file names saved on editor or system crash
–R	set **readonly** mode
–s	suppress interactive feedback
–t *tag*	edit file with *tag* and position cursor at its definition
–v	invoke **vi**
–x	edit encrypted file; prompt for a key to use for encrypting and decrypting text

expr - Evaluate Expression Arguments (PROG)

$ expr *arguments*

Description:

The **expr** command evaluates *arguments* as an expression. Expression tokens must be separated with blanks. Special characters must be escaped. Integer arguments can be preceded by a minus sign to indicate a negative number.

Operators:

Special characters that need to be escaped are preceded by "\." Operators are listed in order of increasing precedence, with operators of equal precedence listed together.

exp1\| *exp2*return *exp1* if it is neither null nor **0**, else return *exp2*

exp1 **\&** *exp2*
return *exp1* if neither null nor **0**, else return **0**

exp1 \<, \<=, =, !=, \>=, \> *exp2*
return the result of the integer or string comparison

exp1 +, –, *, /, % *exp2*
return the result of the arithmetic operation

exp1 : *exp2* return the result on the number of matched characters between *exp1* and *exp2*

exp integer or string; regular expression for matching

Examples:

Display the number of characters in **VAR**

$ expr $VAR : ".*"

Add 1 to **COUNTER**

$ COUNTER=`expr $COUNTER + 1`

exstr – Extract Strings from C Source Files (PROG)

$ exstr *files*

$ exstr –e *files*

$ exstr –r [**–d**] *files*

Description:

The **exstr** command replaces strings from C language source files with calls to the message retrieval function.

Options:

–d	display string if message retrieval fails
–e	include positional information in the extraction
–r	replace strings w/message retrieval function calls

Examples:

Display strings from **dmenu.c**

$ exstr dmenu.c

face – Framed Access Command Environment (MISC)

$ face [*options*] [*files*]

Description:

The **face** command provides a framed access environment for command execution.

Options:

–a *file*	use *file* as alias file
–c *file*	use *file* as FMLI command file
–i *file*	use *file* as initialization file

factor - Factor a Number (MISC)

$ factor [*number*]

Description:

The **factor** command displays the factors of *number*. If not specified, *number* is read from standard input.

Diagnostics:

ouch	displayed on out of range or invalid input

false - Return Unsuccessful Exit Status (MISC)

$ false

Description:

The **false** command returns a unsuccessful (or non-zero) exit status.

fgrep - Search Files for Patterns (FILE)

$ fgrep [*options*] '*string*' [*files*]

Description:

The **fgrep** command displays lines in *files* that contain *string*. Special characters like **$**, *, [, ^, |, (,), and \ are interpreted literally, but should be enclosed in quotes.

Options:

–b	precede each line with the block number
–c	display only a count of matching lines
–e *str*	search for string *str* that begins with –
–f *file*	get strings from *file*
–i	ignore case of letters during comparisons
–l	display only names of files with matching lines
–n	display the output with line numbers
–v	display all lines, except those that match *string*
–x	display exact matching lines only
files	read standard input if no *files* are specified

Examples:

Display number of lines in **file** that contain **(408)**

$ fgrep –c '(408)' file

Display number of lines in **file1** that do not contain **[3]**

$ fgrep –c –v '[3]' file

file - Determine File Type (FILE, BSD)

$ file [*options*] *files*

$ /usr/ucb/file *files*

Description:

The **file** command identifies the type of *files*.

Options:

–c	check magic file for format errors
–f *file*	check the files in *file*
–h	do not follow symbolic links
–m *file*	use *file* as alternate magic file (default **/etc/magic**)

Examples:

Check the file type of **/usr/local/bin/autozap**

$ file /usr/local/bin/autozap

find - Find Files (**FILE**)

$ find *pathname-list options*

Description:

The **find** command recursively descends directories in *pathname list* and searches for files that match *options*.

Options:

–atime *n* true if *file* has been accessed in *n* days

–ctime *n* true if *file* has been changed in *n* days

–depth search for files before directories

–exec *cmd* **\;**
true if *cmd* returns zero exit status. If *cmd* is **{}**, it is replaced with current pathname. An escaped semi-colon must be given after *cmd*.

–follow always true; follow symbolic links

–fstype *type* true if file system is of the given type ***

–group *name*
true if *file* belongs to the group *name* (group name or ID)

–inum *n* true if file has inode numbe *n*

–links *n* true if *file* has *n* links

–local true if *file* resides on the local system

–mount restrict the search to current file system or file system that contains the given directory

–mtime *n* true if *file* has been modified in *n* days

–name *file* true if *file* matches the current file. Special characters should be escaped to avoid interpretation by the shell.

–newer *file* true if the current file is newer than *file*

–nogroup true if file group not in **/etc/group** file

–nouser true if file owner not in **/etc/passwd** file

–ok *cmd* interactive **–exec** option (*cmd* is executed if the invoker responds to the prompt with **y**)

–perm [–]*onum*
true if file permissions match octal *onum*. If *–onum* is given, only set bits in *onum* are compared with file permissions.

–print display the current pathname

–prune always true; do not search below current directory

–size *n* true if *file* is *n* blocks long (512 bytes/block)

–size *nc* true if *file* is *n* characters long

–type *c* true if *file* matches the file type *c*, where *c* can be:

b	block special	**p**	fifo (named pipe)
c	character special	**l**	symbolic link
d	directory	**f**	plain file

–user *name*
true if *file* is owned by *name* (login name of a user ID)

\\(*exp*\\) true if *exp* is true; used for grouping

!*exp* true if *exp* is not true

exp1 exp2 true if both *exp1* and *exp2* are true

exp1 **–o** *exp2*
true if either *exp* or *exp2* are true

n	specifies the number of days where:	
	+*n*	more than *n* days
	–*n*	less than *n* days
	n	exactly *n* days

Examples:

List the names of all directories under **/usr**

$ find /usr –type d –print

Remove all files that belong to **jo** or **mo**

$ find / \(–user jo –o –user mo \) –exec rm {} \;

Backup files that have been modified in the last 24 hours

$ find / –mtime –1 | cpio –oBc >/dev/rst0

List all files owned by root that have the set-UID bit set

$ find / –user root –perm –4000 –print

List files with no owner or group from password or group

$ find / \(–nouser –o –nogroup \) –print

finger - Display Information about Users (MISC, BSD)

$ finger [*options*] [*names*]

$ finger [**–l**] *user@host*

$ /usr/ucb/finger [**–lmps**] [*names*]

Description:

The **finger** command displays the login name, full name, terminal name, write status, idle and login time. If write permission is denied, a * is displayed before terminal name.

Options:

–b	do not display user's home directory and shell
–f	do not display header in output
–h	do not display **.project** file
–l	display in long output format
–m	match arguments only on login name
–p	suppress printing of **.plan** files
–q	display in quick output format
–s	display in short output format
–w	same as **–s**, except do not display full name
names	account name, first name, or last name

Examples:

Display information about **sysadm@memh1**

$ finger –l sysadm@memh1

Display information in long format for all users

$ finger –l

fmli – Invoke FMLI (MISC)

$ fmli [*options*] *files*

Description:

The **fmli** command invokes the Form and Menu Language Interpreter and opens the frames from files.

Options:

–a *file*	use aliases from *file*; (format *alias=pathname*)
–c *file*	use FMLI commands from *file*
–i *file*	initialize application characteristics from *file*

Examples:

\# Invoke **fmli** with initial setting from **init.file**

$ fmli –i init.file Menu.start

fmt - Format Text to Approximately 72 Characters (FILE, BSD)

$ fmt [*options*] [*files*]

$ /usr/ucb/fmt [*files*]

Description:

The **fmt** command formats *files* or **stdin** so that the text lines contain as close to 72 characters as possible. Lines beginning with "**.**" or "**From:**" are not filled.

Options:

–c	preserve indentation of first two lines within paragraph, and align left margin of each line.
–s	split lines only
–w *n*	fill output lines up to *n* columns (default **72**)

Examples:

\# Format **rep.out** and set width to 55 lines

$ fmt –w 55 rep.out

fmtmsg – Display Message (MISC)

$ fmtmsg [*options*] *text*

Description:

The **fmtmsg** command displays a formatted message.

Options:

–a *action* — *action* describes first step in error recovery process (preceded by "**TO FIX:**")

–c *class* — describes source of message; *class* can be:

firm	source of condition is firmware
hard	source of condition is hardware
soft	source of condition is software

–l *label* — identify source of message with *label*

–s *sev* — indicates severity of the error; *sev* can be:

error	application detected a fault
halt	fault detected and is halting
info	application is providing information about a condition not in error
warn	application is providing information about an unusual condition

–t *tag* — *tag* contains an identifier for the message

–u *subclass*

define message and direct display of the message; *subclass* can be:

appl	condition originated in application

console	display message on system console
nrecov	application will not recover
opsys	message originated in kernel
print	display message on standard error
recov	application will recover from condition
util	condition originated in utility

text string that describes condition

Variables:

MSGVERB
colon-separated list of message keywords; can be **action**, **label**, **severity**, **tag**, or **text**

SEV_LEVEL
colon-separated list error descriptions with format:
description=severity-keyword, level, string
severity-keyword is string used with **–s** option, *level* can be greater than **4** (**0-4** reserved)

fold - Fold Long Lines into Shorter Lines (FILE, BSD)

$ fold [**–w** *n*] [*files*]
$ /usr/ucb/fold [–*n*] [*files*]

Description:

The **fold** command displays files with lines longer than the *n* or default width broken out onto multiple lines.

Options:

–w *n*	set output width to *n* (default **80**)
–*n*	set output width to *n* (obsolete option - default **80**)
files	read **stdin** if no *files* specified

Examples:

Display **uucp** log output; set maximum width to 45 lines
$ uulog | fold –45

from - Identify Mail Sender (BSD)

$ **/usr/ucb/rom** [**–s** *name*] [*user*]

Description:

The **from** command displays mail message header.

Options:

–s *user*	display header lines for mail messages from user
user	examine the mailbox for *user*

ftp – Transfer Files (FILE, BSD)

$ ftp [*options*] [*host*]

Description:

The **ftp** command transfers files to and from a remote system.

Options:

–d	enable debugging
–g	disable file name expansion
–i	do not prompt during multiple file transfers

–n do not attempt auto-login. If not given, the **.netrc** file is checked for account name for remote system. If no account name exists, invoker is prompted for login to use. (default local login)

–v show host responses and transfer statistics

Commands:

account [*password*]
supply a password (default prompt for one)

append *file1*[*file2*]
append local *file1* to remote *file2*. If no *file2* given, use local *file1*.

ascii set file transfer type to ascii (default)

bell sound bell after each file transfer completes

binary set file transfer type to binary

bye exit from **ftp**

case toggle remote file name case mapping for **mget**. If on, remote file names mapped to lower case.

cd *dir* change directory on remote system to *dir*

cdup change directory on remote system to the parent directory

close terminate current **ftp** session

cr toggle carriage return stripping

delete *file* delete *file* on remote system

debug [*n*] set debugging level to *n*

debug toggle debugging mode

dir [*directory*] [*file*]
list contents of remote directory. Put output in *file*.

disconnect terminate current **ftp** session

form *format*
set file transfer type to *format* (default **file**)

get *file1* [*file2*]
copy remote *file1* to local *file1*. If no *file2* given, use remote *file1*.

glob toggle filename expansion for **mdelete**, **mget**, **mput**

hash toggle hash-sign printing for data block transfers

help [*cmd*] display help information for all commands or *cmd*.

lcd [*dir*] change local working directory to *dir* (default **$HOME**)

ls [*directory*] [*file*]
put listing of remote *directory* contents in *file*. If no *file* given, list contents on **stdout**. (default current remote working directory)

macdef *macro*
define *macro*

mdelete [*files*]
delete remote *files*

mdir *files file2*
put listing of remote *files* in local *file1*. Prompt for files if none specified.

mget *files* perform filename expansion on remote *files* and execute **get** for each file.

mkdir *dir* create remote directory *dir*

mls *files file1*
put short listing of remote *files* in local *file1*. Prompt for files if none specified.

mode [*mode*]
set file transfer mode to **stream**

mput *files* expand * in list of local files and execute **put** on each file produced. Process each file according to **case**, **ntrans**, and **nmap** settings, then transfer to the local directory.

nmap unset filename mapping

nmap [*pattern1 pattern2*]
set filename mapping for **get**, **mget**, **mput**, and **put**

ntrans unset filename character translation

ntrans [*str1* [*str2*]]
set filename character translation. Characters in filenames from *str1* replaced with corresponding characters from *str2* for **get**, **mget**, **mput**, and **put**.

open *host* [*port*]
establish a connection to *host* through *port*

prompt toggle interactive prompting (default enabled)

proxy *cmd* execute **ftp** command on a secondary connection

put *file1* [*file2*]
copy local *file1* to remote *file2*. If no *file2* given, use remote *file1*.

pwd display remote current working directory name

quit exit from **ftp**

quote *args* send *args* to remote server

recv *file1* [*file2*]
copy remote *file2* to local *file1*. If no *file2* given, use remote *file1*.

remotehelp [*cmd*]
request help for all or *cmd* from the remote server

rename [*file1*] [*file2*]
rename remote ***file1*** to remote *file2*

reset clear the screen

rmdir *dir* remove the remote directory *dir*

runique toggle file storing on local system. If a file already exists, then **.1** is appended to the name. If this file exists, a **.2** is appended to the file name. (max **.99**)

send *file1* [*file2*]
copy local *file1* to remote *file2*. If no *file2* given, use remote *file1*.

sendport toggle the use of port commands

status display the current **ftp** status

struct [*name*]
set file transfer structure to *name* (default **stream**)

sunique toggle file storing on remote system with unique file names

tenex set the file transfer type to talk to TENEX systems

trace toggle packet tracing

type display the current file transfer type

type [*type*] set the file transfer type (default **ASCII**)

user *user* [*password*] [*account*]
identifies invoker to the server. The invoker is prompted for password and account if needed.

verbose toggle verbose mode

$*macro* execute *macro*

! escape to an interactive shell

!*cmd* escape to the shell and execute *cmd*

? [*cmd*] display help information for *cmd*

Files:

.netrc	contains login and initialization information:
	machine *name* — set remote system *name*
	login *name* — set user name for remote login
	password *str* — set password for remote login
	account *str* s — et account for remote login
	macdef *name* — define a macro *name*

Examples:

\# Open **ftp** connection to 130.26.4.1; do not auto-login

$ ftp –n 130.26.4.1

gcore – Get Core Images of Processes (PROG)

$ gcore [**–o** *file*] *process-id*

Description:

The **gcore** command creates a core image of a process.

Options:

–o *file*	put output in *file.process-id*

Examples:

\# Create core image for process **4271**

$ gcore 4271

gencat – Generate Formatted Message Catalogue (MISC)

$ gencat [**–m**] *catfile msgfile*

Description:

The **gencat** command merges the message text source file *msgfile* into a formatted message database *catfile*. If *catfile* is non-existent, a new file is created.

Options:

–m	build *catfile* that is compatible with other versions

get - Get a Version of an SCCS File (SCCS)

$ get [*options*] **s.***file* **. . .**

Description:

The **get** command retrieves a version of a file from **s.***file*.

Options:

–a*n*	retrieve delta sequence *n* (has precedence over **–r**)
–b	create a new branch; ignored if the **b** flag is not present; (only with **–e**; see **admin**)
–c*date*	do not include deltas created after *date*
–e	make retrieved text writable (used to make a change to the SCCS file via **delta**)
–g	suppress text retrieval (create **l.***file*)
–i*list*	retrieve deltas from *list* (single, comma-separated or – separated deltas)
–k	suppress replacement of ID keywords

–l	write a delta summary to **l.***file*
–lp	do not create **l.***file* (send output to **stdout**)
–m	prepend delta to retrieved text line
–n	precede retrieved text line with **%M%** keyword
–p	send the output to **stdout** (no **g.***file* created)
–r*n*	retrieve delta *n*
–s	suppress non-fatal diagnostic messages
–t	retrieve the newest delta in the release
–w*text*	replace *text* for all **%W%** keywords
–x*list*	do not retrieve deltas from *list* (single, comma-separated or – separated deltas)
files	file names beginning with **s.**, **–**, or directory names. If *files* is a directory, then all files in directory beginning with **s.** are processed. If *files* is **–**, read file names from **stdin**.

Examples:

Retrieve delta **1.7** of **s.file** and suppress messages

$ get –r1.7 s.file

Retrieve highest delta for **s.hello.c** in release **3**

$ get –e –t –r3 s.hello.c

Display version **3.2** of **s.file** on standard output

$ get –p –r3.2 s.file1 | pg

getopts - Parse Command Options (MISC)

$ getopts *optstring option* [*args*]

Description:

The **getopts** command parses command-line options in shell scripts.

Options:

optstring	string of valid option letters. If a letter is followed by a colon, it indicates that the option has an argument that may or may not be separated from it by white space. The option **––** is used to indicate end of options.

Variables:

OPTARG	contains the option argument
OPTIND	contains the index of the next option

gettxt – Get Text String from Message Database (MISC)

$ gettxt *msgfile:msgnum* [*default-msg*]

Description:

The **gettxt** command retrieves a text string from a file.

Options:

default-msg	default string to use if no message found
msgfile	file from **/usr/lib/locale/***locale***/LC_MESSAGES** directory (default **$LC_MESSAGES** or **$LANG**)
msgnum	message number to retrieve

Examples:

Retrieve seventh message; display **Error!** on error

$ gettxt UX:7 "Error!\n"

grep, groups, head

grep - Search Files for Patterns (FILE)

$ grep [*options*] '*expression*' [*files*]

Description:

The **grep** command displays lines in *files* that match the given limited regular expression patterns.

Options:

–b	precede each line with the block number
–c	display number of lines that contain *expression*
–i	ignore case of letters during comparisons
–l	display only names of files with matching lines once
–n	display output with line numbers
–s	do not display error messages
–v	display all lines, except those matching *expression*
expr	limited regular expression (see **ed**)
files	read standard input of no *files* are specified

Examples:

Display the line numbers in **docs*** that contain **Chapter**

$ grep –n 'Chapter' docs*

Display file names that do not contain "**.c**"

$ ls | grep –v '.c'

Display users that are using the Korn shell

$ grep ':/bin/ksh$' /etc/passwd

Show number of lines in **file** that contain **ix**; ignore case

$ grep –c 'ix' file

groups – Display Group Membership (MISC, BSD)

$ groups [*user*]

$ /usr/ucb/groups [*user*]

Description:

The **groups** command displays the groups to which the invoker or *user* belong.

head - Display First Lines of a File (FILE, BSD)

$ head [*n*] [*files*]

$ /usr/ucb/head [*n*] [*files*]

Description:

The **head** command displays first 10 or *n* of lines of *files*.

Options:

–n	display first *n* lines (default **10**)

Examples:

Display the first 50 lines of **msg.log**

$ head –50 msg.log

help - Provide SCCS Help (SCCS)

$ **help** [*arguments*]

Description:

The **help** command provides assistance for SCCS commands and message numbers.

Options:

arguments message numbers or command names

Examples:

Provide information about the **admin** command
$ help admin

hostid - Display Current Host System Identifier (MISC)

$ **hostid**

hostid *id* | *name*

Description:

The **hostid** command displays the host id in hex. The super-user can set the hostid by using a hex argument or host name.

hostname - Display Host Name (MISC)

$ **hostname**

hostname *name*

Description:

The **hostname** command displays the current host name. The super-user can set the current host name.

iconv – Convert Code Set (MISC)

$ **codeset –f** *from* **–t** *to* [*file*]

Description:

The **iconv** command converts characters or sequences of characters in *file* from one code set to another.

Options:

–f *from*	identifies source code set
–t *to*	identifies target code set
file	if no *file* given, read standard input

Examples:

Convert **msg** from **8859** to **646it** and display result
$ iconv –f 8859 –t 646it msg

id - Display Names and User/Group ID's (MISC)

$ **id** [–a]

Description:

The **id** command displays user ID, group ID, and name of the invoking process. The effective and real ID's are also displayed if they are different.

Options:

–a	displays groups to which invoking process of user belongs

Examples:

Set the variable **WHO** to your name

$ WHO=`id | sed –e 's/).*//' | sed –e 's/.*(//'`

install - Install Files (**MISC**)

$ /usr/sbin/install [*options*] *file* [*dirs*]

$ **/usr/ucb/install** [*options*] *file* [*dirs*]

Description:

The **install** command installs *file* in a target directory. If no directories are given, then *file* is installed in **/usr/usr/bin**, **/usr/usr/usr/bin**, **/etc**, **/usr/usr/lib**, or **/usr/usr/usr/lib**.

Options:

–c *dir*	install in *dir* if *file* is non-existent
–f *dir*	force installation in *dir* to mode **755**, owner **bin**
–g *group*	set group ID of file to *group* (super-user only)
–i	ignore default directory search list
–m *mode*	change mode of file to *mode* (default **755**)
–o	copy original file to **OLD***file* before overwriting
–o *user*	change ownerof *dest* to *user* (default **root**) (**BSD**)
–s	do not print non-error messages
–s	strip dest after installation (**BSD**)
–u *user*	set owner of file to *user* (super-user only)

Examples:

Install new version of **autologoff** in **/etc** and save original

$ /usr/sbin/install –o autologoff /etc

Install **rn** in **/bin**; set owner and group to **news**, mode **755**

$ /usr/sbin/install –m755 –u news –g news rn /bin

ipcrm - Remove IPC Facilities (**SYSTEM**)

$ ipcrm [*options*]

Description:

The **ipcrm** command removes the specified IPC facility.

Options:

–m *n*	remove shared memory id *n*
–M *n*	remove shared memory id created with key *n*
–q *n*	remove message queue id *n*
–Q *n*	remove message queue id created with key *n*
–s *n*	remove semaphore id *n*
–S *n*	remove semaphore id created with key *n*

Examples:

Remove shared memory identifier **1201**

$ ipcrm –m 1201

ipcs – Report IPC Facilities Status (MISC)

$ ipcs [*options*]

Description:

The **ipcs** command displays status information about IPC facilities. If no *options* are given, information for all IPC facilities is displayed.

Options:

–a	use all format options (same as **–b**, **–c**, **–o**, **–p**, **–t**)
–b	display information on largest allowable size
–c	display login and group name of creator
–C *file*	use *file* instead of **/dev/kmem**
–m	display active shared memory information
–N *file*	use *file* instead of **/unix**
–o	display outstanding usage information
–p	display process number information
–q	display message queues information
–s	display active semaphores information
–t	display time information

Examples:

\# Display login and group name of the semaphores creator

$ ipcs –s –c

ismpx - Return Window Terminal State (MISC)

$ ismpx [–s]

Description:

The **ismpx** command displays **yes** and returns **0** if invoked under **layers**, otherwise it displays **no** and returns **1**.

Options:

–s	do not display messages; return exit status only

join - Relational Database Operator (MISC)

$ join [*options*] *file1 file2*

Description:

The **join** command forms a join of two relations from *file1* and *file2*. The output is one line for each pair of lines in the given files that have the same join fields.

Options:

–a*n*	create line for unpairable lines from file *n* (*n* can be **1** or **2**)
–e *str*	replace empty output fields with string *str*
–j*n m*	join on field *m* of file *n*. If *n* is missing, use *mth* field in each file.
–o *list*	display fields from *list;list* format: *n.m* (field *m* of file *n*)
–t *c*	set field separator to *c*
files	read standard input if *file1* or *file2* is –

Examples:

\# Display lines in **Dialcodes** and **Systems** that have same
\# phone field and display abbreviation field from **Dialcodes**

$ join –j1 2 –j2 5 –o 1.1 Dialcodes Systems

jsh – (See **SH**)

jterm - Reset a Layer (**MISC**)

$ jterm

Description:

The **jterm** command resets a layer of a windowing terminal after downloading a terminal program.

jwin - Display Layer Size (**MISC**)

$ jwin

Description:

The **jwin** command displays the width and height of the layer associated with the current process.

keylogin - Decrypt a Secret Key (**MISC**)

$ keylogin

Description:

The **keylogin** command prompts for a password to decrypt a key.

keylogout - Delete a Secret Key (**MISC**)

$ keylogout

Description:

The **keylogout** command deletes the secret key.

Options:

–f forget the root key

kill - Terminate a Process (**SYSTEM**)

$ kill [*–signal*] *process-ID . . .*

$ kill [*–signal*] *–process-group-ID . . .*

$ kill –l

Description:

The **kill** command sends *signal* to the specified processes. If no *signal* is given, send signal **15**. The signal may be numeric or symbolic. Only a process owned by the current user can be signalled, unless invoker is the super-user.

Options:

–l display a list of valid signal names

–process-group-ID
send *signal* to all processes with *progress-group-ID*. If *process-group-ID* is **0**, send *signal* to all current processes.

process-ID send *signal* to processes associated with *process-ID*. If *process-ID* is **0**, send *signal* to all current processes.

Examples:

\# Terminate process 1197 and 1203

$ kill –9 1197 1203

\# Terminate all current processes started since login

$ kill –9 0

ksh - Korn Shell (**MISC**)

$ ksh [*options*] [*args*]

Description:

The **ksh** command is a command language interpreter. It executes commands read from the terminal, and from a file.

Options:

Korn shell options are enabled/disabled on the command-line, or with the **set** command.

–a	automatically export variables that are defined
–b	execute all background jobs at a lower priority
–c *cmds*	read and execute *cmds* (on command-line only)
–e	execute **ERR** trap (if set) on non-zero exit status from any commands
–f	disable file name expansion
–h	make commands tracked aliases when first encountered
–i	execute in interactive mode (command-line only)
–k	put variable assignment arguments in environment
–m	enable job control (system dependent)
–n	read commands without executing them
–o allexport	automatically export variables that are defined
–o bgnice	execute all background jobs at a lower priority
–o emacs	use emacs-style editor for in-line editing
–o errexit	execute **ERR** trap (if set) on non-zero exit status from any commands
–o gmacs	use gmacs-style editor for in-line editing
–o ignoreeof	do not exit on end of file (default **Ctl-d**); use **exit**
–o keyword	put variable assignment arguments in environment
–o markdirs	display trailing / on directory names resulting from file name substitution
–o monitor	enable job control (system dependent)
–o noclobber	stop I/O redirection from truncating existing files
–o noexec	read commands without executing them
–o noglob	disable file name expansion
–o nolog	do not save function definitions in history file
–o nounset	return error on substitution of unset variables
–o privileged	disable processing of **$HOME/.profile**, and use **/etc/suid_profile** instead of **ENV** file
–o trackall	make commands tracked aliases when first encountered
–o verbose	display input lines as they are read
–o vi	use vi-style editor for in-line editing
–o viraw	process each character as it is typed in vi mode
–o xtrace	display commands and arguments as executed

–p disable processing of **$HOME/.profile**, and use **/etc/suid_profile** instead of **ENV** file

–r run a restricted shell (command-line only)

–s read commands from standard input (command-line only)

–t exit after reading and executing one command

–u return error on substitution of unset variables

–v display input lines as they are read

–x display commands and arguments as executed

– disable **–v, –x** flags; don't process remaining flags

Command Execution Format:

cmd1; *cmd2*
execute *cmd1* followed by *cmd2*

cmd & execute *cmd* asynchronously in the background; do not wait for completion

cmd1 | *cmd2*
pass **stdout** of *cmd1* to **stdin** of *cmd2*

cmd1 && *cmd2*
execute *cmd2* if *cmd1* returns successful exit status

cmd1 || *cmd2*
execute *cmd2* if *cmd1* returns unsuccessful exit status

cmd |& execute *cmd* asynchronously with its **stdin** and **stdout** attached to the parent shell; use **read –p/print –p** to manipulate the **stdin/stdout**

cmd \ continue *cmd* onto the next line

{ *cmd* ;} execute *cmd* in the current shell

(*cmd*) execute *cmd* in a subshell

I/O Redirection Operators:

<*file* redirect standard input from *file*

>*file* redirect standard output to *file*. Create *file* if non-existent, else overwrite.

>>*file* append standard output to *file*; create if non-existent.

>|*file* redirect standard output to *file*. Create *file* if non-existent, else overwrite even if **noclobber** is set.

<>*file* open *file* for reading and writing as standard input

<&– close standard input

>&– close standard output

<&*n* redirect standard input from file descriptor *n*

>&*n* redirect standard output to file descriptor *n*

n<*file* redirect file descriptor *n* from *file*

n>*file* redirect file descriptor *n* to *file*

n>>*file* redirect file descriptor *n* to *file*. Create *file* if non-existent, else overwrite.

n>|*file* redirect file descriptor *n* to *file*. Create *file* if non-existent, else overwrite even if **noclobber** is set.

n<&*m* redirect file descriptor *n* from file descriptor *m*

n>&*m* redirect file descriptor *n* to file descriptor *m*

n<>*file* open *file* for reading and writing as file descriptor *n*

n<<*word* redirect to file descriptor *n* until *word* is read

n<<–*word* redirect to file descriptor *n* until *word* is read; ignore leading tabs

n<&– close file descriptor *n* for standard input

n>&–   close file descriptor *n* for standard output

n<&**p**   redirect input from co-process to file descriptor *n*. If *n* is not specified, use standard input.

n>&**p**   redirect output of co-process to file descriptor *n*. If *n* is not specified, use standard output.

Filename Substitution:

?   match any single character

*   match zero or more characters, including null

[**abc**]   match any characters between the brackets

[**x–z**]   match any character or characters in the range **x-z**

[**a–ce–g**]   match any characters in the range **a** to **c**, **e** to **g**

[**!abc**]   match any characters not between the brackets

[**!x–z**]   match any characters not in the range **x** to **z**

.   strings starting with **.** must be explicitly matched

?(*pattern-list*)
  match zero or one occurrence of any *pattern*

*(*pattern-list*)
  match zero or more occurrences of any *pattern*

+(*pattern-list*)
  match one or more occurrence of any *pattern*

@(*pattern-list*)
  match exactly one occurrence of any *pattern*

!(*pattern-list*)
  match anything except any *pattern*

pattern-list   multiple patterns must be separated with a | character

Variable/Attribute Assignment Format:

variable=   declare *variable* and set it to null

typeset *variable*=
  declare *variable* and set it to null. If used within a function, then a local variable is declared.

variable=*value*
  assign *value* to *variable*

typeset *variable*=*value*
  assign *value* to *variable*. If used within a function, then a local variable is declared.

typeset –*attribute variable*=*value*
  assign *attribute* and *value* to *variable*

typeset –*attribute variable*
  assign *attribute* to *variable*

typeset +*attribute variable*
  remove *attribute* from *variable* (except **readonly**)

Variable/Attribute Listing Format:

typeset –*attribute*
  display variable names and values that have *attribute* set

typeset +*attribute*
  display variable names that have *attribute* set

Variable Attribute Assignment Format:

typeset –H *variable*
  set UNIX to host-name file mapping

typeset –i *variable*
set *variable* to be integer type

typeset –i*n variable*
set *variable* to be integer type with base *n*

typeset –l *variable*
set *variable* to lower case

typeset –L *variable*
left justify *variable*; width is given by first assignment

typeset –L*n variable*
left justify *variable*; set field width to *n*

typeset –LZ*n variable*
left justify *variable*; set field width to *n;*strip leading zeros

typeset –r *variable*
set *variable* to be readonly (same as **readonly**)

typeset –R *variable*
right justify *variable*; width is given by first assignment

typeset –R*n variable*
right justify *variable*; set field width to *n*

typeset –RZ*n variable*
right justify *variable*; set field width to *n* and fill with leading zeros

typeset –t *variable*
set user-defined attribute for *variable* (no meaning)

typeset –u *variable*
set *variable* to upper case

typeset –x *variable*
automatically export variable to environment

typeset –Z *variable*
same as **typeset –RZ**

Variable Expansion Format:

${*variable*} value of *variable*

${*#variable*}
length of *variable*

${*variable*:–*word*}
value of *variable* if set and not null, else print *word*. If **:** is omitted, *variable* is only checked if it is set.

${*variable*:=*word*}
value of *variable* if set and not null, else variable is set to *word*, then expanded. If **:** is omitted, *variable* is only checked if it is set.

${*variable*:?}
value of *variable* if set and not null, else print "**variable: parameter null or not set**". If **:** is omitted, *variable* is only checked if it is set.

${*variable*:?*word*}
value of *variable* if set and not null, else print value of *word* and exit. If **:** is omitted, *variable* is only checked if it is set.

${*variable*:+*word*}
value of *word* if *variable* is set and not null, else nothing is substituted. If **:** is omitted, *variable* is only checked if it is set.

${*variable#pattern*}
value of *variable* without the smallest beginning portion that matches *pattern*

${*variable##pattern*}
: value of *variable* without the largest beginning portion that matches *pattern*

${*variable%pattern*}
: value of *variable* without the smallest ending portion that matches *pattern*

${*variable%%pattern*}
: value of *variable* without the largest ending portion that matches *pattern*

Special Parameters:

$#	number of positional parameters
$@	all positional parameters ("**$1**", "**$2**", ..., "**$***n*")
$*	all positional parameters ("**$1 $2** ... **$***n*")
$?	exit status of the last command
$$	process id of the current shell
$–	current options in effect
$!	process id of last background command or co-process

Special Variables:

CDPATH	search path for **cd** when not given full pathname (no default)
COLUMNS	window width for in-line edit mode and **select** command lists (default **80**)
EDITOR	pathname of editor for in-line editing (default **/bin/ed**)
ENV	pathname of environment file (no default)
ERRNO	error number returned by most recently failed system call (system dependent)
FCEDIT	default editor for the **fc** command
FPATH	search path for auto-loaded functions
HISTFILE	pathname of history file (default**$HOME/.sh_history**)
HISTSIZE	number of commands to save in the command history file (default **128**)
HOME	home directory
IFS	internal field separator (default space, tab, newline)
LINES	specifies column length for **select** lists
MAIL	name of mail file
MAILCHECK	specifies how often to check for mail (default **600** seconds)
MAILPATH	search path for mail files (no default)
OLDPWD	previous working directory
OPTARG	value of last **getopts** option argument
OPTIND	index of last **getopts** option argument
PATH	search path for commands (default **/bin:/usr/bin:**)
PPID	process id of the parent shell
PS1	primary prompt string (default $, #)
PS2	secondary prompt string (default >)
PS3	**select** command prompt (default #?)
PS4	debug prompt string (default +)
RANDOM	contains a random number
REPLY	contains **read** input when no variables given
SECONDS	contains number of seconds since Korn shell invocation

SHELL pathname of shell
TERM specifies your terminal type (no default)
TMOUT Korn shell timeout variable (default **0**)
VISUAL pathname of the editor for in-line editing

Array Variable Assignment Format:

variable[0]=*value variable*[1]=*value* ... *variable*[*n*]=*value* ,
set –A *variable value0 value1* ... *valuen* ,
typeset *variable*[0]=*value variable*[1]=*value* ... *variable*[n]=*value*
  assign values to array variable elements

set +A *variable value0 value1* ... *valuen*
  reassign values to array variable elements

typeset –*attributes variable*[0]=*value variable*[1]=*value* ... *variable*[*n*]=*value*
  assign *attributes* and values to array variable elements

typeset –*attributes variable*
  assign *attributes* to array variable

typeset + *attributes variable*
  remove *attributes* from array variable (except **readonly**)

Array Variable Evaluation:

${*array*}, $*array*
  array element zero

${*array*[*n*]} array element *n*

${*array*[*]}, ${*array*[@]}
  all elements of an array

${#*array*[*]}, ${#*array*[@]}
  number of array elements

${#*array*[*n*]}
  length of array element *n*

Misc Substitution:

$(*command*)
  replace with standard output of *command*

$((*arithmetic-expression*))
  replace with result of *arithmetic-expression*

$(<*file*) replace with contents of *file*

`*cmd*` replace with standard output of *cmd* (provided for compatibility with the Bourne shell)

~ replace with **$HOME**

~*user* replace with home directory of *user*

~– replace with **$OLDPWD** (previous directory)

~+ replace with **$PWD** (current directory)

Quoting:

'...' remove the meaning of enclosed characters except '

"..." remove special meaning of enclosed characters except $, ', and \

c remove special meaning of character *c*

`*cmd*` replace with standard output of the given command

Vi Input Mode Commands:

#, <BACKSPACE>
  delete the previous character

Ctl-d terminate the Korn shell

Ctl-v escape the next character

Ctl-w	delete the previous word
Ctl-x, @	kill the entire line
<ENTER>	execute the current line
\	escape the next *erase* or *kill* character

Vi Motion Edit Commands:

[*n*]**h**, [*n*]<BACKSPACE>	move left one character
[*n*]l, [*n*]<SPACE>	move forward one character
[*n*]**b**	move backward one word
[*n*]**B**	move backward one word; ignore punctuation
[*n*]**w**	move forward one word
[*n*]**W**	move forward one word; ignore punctuation
[*n*]**e**	move to end of the next word
[*n*]**E**	move to end of next word; ignore punctuation
[*n*]**f***c*	move forward to character *c*
[*n*]**F***c*	move backward to character *c*
[*n*]**t***c*	move forward to character before character *c*
[*n*]**T***c*	move backward to character before character *c*
[*n*]**;**	repeat last **f**, **F**, **t**, or **T** command
[*n*]**,**	repeat last **f**, **F**, **t**, or **T** command, but in opposite direction
0	move cursor to start of line
^	move cursor to first non-blank character in line
$	move cursor to end of line

Vi Search/Edit History Commands:

[*n*]**G**	get last command (or command *n*)
[*n*]**j**, [*n*]+	get next command from history file
[*n*]**k**, [*n*]–	get previous command from history file
n	repeat last / or ? search
N	repeat last / or ? search, except in opposite direction
/string	search backward in history file for command that matches *string*
?string	search forward in history file for command that matches *string*

Vi Text Modification Commands:

a	add text after the current character
A	append text to end of the current line
[*n*]**c***X*, **c**[*n*]*X*	change current character up to position *X*
[*n*]**d***X*, **d**[*n*]*X*	delete current character up to position defined by *X*
[*n*]**y***X*, **y**[*n*]*X*	copy current char up to position *X* into buffer
X	define ending cursor position for **c**, **d**, or **y**
	b — backwards to beginning of word
	e — cursor to end of current word
	w — cursor to beginning of next word
	W B E — same as **w b e**, except ignore punctuation
	0 — before cursor to end of current line
	$ — cursor to end of current line
C	change current character to end of line

D	delete current character through end of line
i	insert text left of the current character
I	insert text before beginning of line
[*n*]**p**	put previously yanked/deleted text after cursor
[*n*]**P**	put previously yanked/deleted text before cursor
[*n*]**r***c*	replace current character with *c*
R	replace text from cursor to <ESCAPE>
S	delete entire line and enter input mode
yy	copy current line into buffer
[*n*]**x**	delete current character
[*n*]**X**	delete previous character
[*n*]**.**	repeat last text modification command
[*n*]~	toggle case of the current character
[*n*]_	append last word of previous **ksh** command
\	replace current word with the filename that matches *word**. For unique matches, append a / to directories and " " (space) for files.

Vi Other Edit Commands:

u	undo last text modification command
U	undo all text mod. commands on current line
[*n*]**v**	return output of the **fc –e** command
Ctl-l	redisplay current line
Ctl-j	execute current line
Ctl-m	execute current line
#	insert a # (comment) at beginning of current line
=	list the files that match the current *word**
*	replace current word with files that match *word**
@_*c*	insert value of alias *c*

Emacs/Gmacs In-Line Editor Commands:

Ctl-b	move left one character
Ctl-f	move right one character
Esc-b	move left one word
Esc-f	move right one word
Ctl-a	move to beginning of line
Ctl-e	move to end of line
Ctl-h	delete preceding character
Ctl-x	delete the entire line
Ctl-k	delete from cursor to end of line
Ctl-d	delete current character
Esc-d	delete current word
Ctl-w	delete from cursor to mark
Ctl-y	undo last delete (w/**Esc-p**)
Ctl-p	get previous command from history file
Ctl-n	get next command from history file
Ctl-o	execute current command line and get next command line
Ctl-r*str*	search back in history file for command that contains *str*
Ctl-c	change current character to upper case
Esc-c	change current word to upper case
Esc-l	change current character to lower case
Esc-p	save to buffer from cursor to mark

Esc-<SPACE>, **Ctl-@** — mark current location

Ctl-l — redisplay current line

Ctl-]*c* — move cursor forward to character *c*

Ctl-xCtl-x — interchange the cursor and mark

erase — delete previous character

Esc-Ctl-h — delete previous word

Esc-h — delete previous word

Ctl-t — transpose current and next character (**emacs**)

Ctl-t — transpose two previous characters (**gmacs**)

Ctl-j — execute current line

Ctl-m — execute current line

Esc-< — get oldest command line

Esc-> — get previous command line

Esc-*n* — define parameter *n* the next command (command can be **Ctl-c**, **Ctl-d**, **Ctl-k**, **Ctl-n**, **Ctl-p**, **Ctl-r**, **Esc-.**, **Ctl-]***c*, **Esc-_**, **Esc-b**, **Esc-c**, **Esc-d**, **Esc-f**, **Esc-h**, **Esc-l**, **Esc-Ctl-h**)

Esc-*c* — insert value of alias _*c* (*c* cannot be **b**, **c**, **d**, **f**, **h**, **l**, or **p**)

Esc-., **Esc-_** — insert last word of previous command

Esc-Esc — replace current word with filename that matches *word**. For unique matches, append a / to directories and " " (space) for files

Esc-= — list files that match current *word*

Ctl-u — multiply parameter of next command by 4

\ — escape the next character

Ctl-v — display the version of the Korn shell

Esc-# — insert a # (comment) at beginning of current line

Job Control Commands:

bg — put current stopped job in the background

bg %*n* — put stopped job *n* in the background

fg — move current background job into the foreground

fg %*n* — move background job *n* into the foreground

jobs — display status of all jobs

jobs –l — display status of all jobs and their process ids

jobs –p — display process ids of all jobs

kill –l — list all valid signal names

kill [–*signal*] %*n* — send specified signal to job *n* (default **9**)

set –m, **set –o monitor** — enable job control

stty [–]**tostop** — allow/prevent background jobs from generating output

wait — wait for all background jobs to complete

wait %*n* — wait for background job *n* to complete

Ctl-z — stop the current job

Job Name Format:

%*n* — job *n*

%+, %% — current job

%– — previous job

%*string* — job whose name begins with *string*

%?*string* — job that matches part or all of *string*

Arithmetic Commands:

let "*arithmetic-expression*" ,
((*arithmetic-expression*))
: evaluate arithmetic expression

integer *variable*
: declare an integer variable

integer *variable=integer-value*
: declare an integer variable and set it to a value

integer *variable="arithmetic-assignment-expression"*
: declare an integer variable and assign it the value of the *arithmetic-assignment-expression*

typeset –i*n* *variable*[=*value*]
: declare base *n* integer variable (optionally assign a value)

Arithmetic Operators:

- – unary minus
- ! logical negation
- ~ bitwise negation
- *, /, % multiplication, division, remainder (modulo)
- +, – addition, subtraction
- <<, >> left shift, right shift
- <=, < less than or equal to, less than
- >=, > greater than or equal to, greater than
- = =, != equal to, not equal to
- & bitwise AND
- ^ bitwise exclusive OR
- | bitwise OR
- && logical AND
- || logical OR
- = assignment
- *=, /=, %= multiply assign, divide assign, modulo assign
- +=, –= increment, decrement
- <<=, >>= left shift assign, right shift assign
- &=, ^=, |= bitwise AND assign, bitwise exclusive OR assign, bitwise OR assign
- (...) grouping (used to override precedence rules)

Alias Commands:

alias display a list of aliases and their values

alias *name* display the value for alias *name*

alias *name='value'*
: create an alias *name* set to *value*

alias –t display a list of tracked aliases

alias –t *name='value'*
: create a tracked alias *name* set to *value*

alias –x display a list of exported aliases

alias –x *name='value'*
: create an exported alias *name* set to *value*

unalias *name*
: remove the alias *name*

Some Preset Aliases:

Alias	Value	Definition
autoload	**typeset –fu**	define an autoloading function
echo	**print –**	display arguments
functions	**typeset –f**	display list of functions
hash	**alias –t –**	display list of tracked aliases
history	**fc –l**	list commands from history file
integer	**typeset –i**	declare integer variable
r	**fc –e –**	re-execute previous command
stop	**kill –STOP**	suspend job
type	**whence –v**	display information about commands

[[...]] String Operators:

–n *string* true if length of *string* is not zero

–o *option* true if *option* is set

–z *string* true if length of *string* is zero

string1 = *string2*
true if *string1* is equal to *string2*

string1 != *string2*
true if *string1* is not equal to *string2*

string = *pattern*
true if *string* matches *pattern*

string != *pattern*
true if *string* does not match *pattern*

string1 < *string2*
true if *string1* is less than *string2*

string1 > *string2*
true if *string1* is greater than *string2*

[[...]] File Operators:

–a *file* true if *file* exists

–b *file* true if *file* exists and is a block special file

–c *file* true if *file* exists and is a character special file

–d *file* true if *file* exists and is a directory

–f *file* true if *file* exists is a regular file

–g *file* true if *file* exists and setgid bit is set

–G *file* true if *file* exists and group id matches current effective group id

–k *file* true if *file* exists and sticky bit is set

–L *file* true if *file* exists and is a symbolic link

–O *file* true if *file* exists and is owned by effective user id

–p *file* true if *file* exists and is a fifo special file or a pipe

–r *file* true if *file* exists and is readable

–s *file* true if *file* exists and size is greater than zero

–S *file* true if *file* exists and is a socket

–t *n* true if file descriptor *n* is open and associated with a terminal device

–u *file* true if *file* exists and its set user-id bit is set

–w *file* true if *file* exists and is writable

–x *file* true if *file* exists and is executable. If *file* is a directory, then true indicates directory is readable.

file1 **–ef** *file2*
true if *file1* and *file2* exist and refer to same file

file1 **–nt** *file2*
true if *file1* exists and is newer than *file2*

file1 **–ot** *file2*
true if *file1* exists and is older than *file2*

[[...]] Integer Operators:

exp1 **–eq** *exp2*
true if *exp1* is equal to *exp2*

exp1 **–ne** *exp2*
true if *exp1* is not equal to *exp2*

exp1 **–le** *exp2*
true if *exp1* is less than or equal to *exp2*

exp1 **–lt** *exp2*
true if *exp1* is less than *exp2*

exp1 **–ge** *exp2*
true if *exp1* is greater than or equal to *exp2*

exp1 **–gt** *exp2*
true if *exp1* is greater than *exp2*

Other [[...]] Operators:

!*expression* true if *expression* is false

(*expression*)
true if *expression* is true; used to group expressions

[[*expression1* && *expression2*]]
true if both *expression1* and *expression2* are true

[[*expression1* || *expression2*]]
true either *expression1* or *expression2* are true

Control Commands:

case *value* **in**
pattern1) *commands1* **;;**
pattern2) *commands2* **;;**
. . .
patternn) *commandsn* **;;**
esac
Execute commands associated with *pattern* that matches *value*.

for *variable* **in** *word1 word2 . . . wordn*
do
commands
done
Execute *commands* once for each *word*, setting *variable* to successive *words* each time.

for *variable*
do
commands
done
Execute *commands* once for each positional parameter, setting *variable* to positional parameters each time.

if *command1*
then
commands
fi
Execute *commands* if *command1* returns a zero exit status.

if *command1*
then
commands2
else
commands3
fi

Execute *commands2* if *commands1* returns a zero exit status, otherwise execute *commands3*.

if *command1*
then
commands
elif *command2*
then
commands
. . .
elif *commandn*
then
commands
else
commands
fi

If *command1* returns a zero exit status, or *command2* returns a zero exit status, or *commandn* returns a zero exit status, then execute the *commands* corresponding to the **if/elif** that returned a zero exit status. Otherwise, if all the **if/elif** commands return a non-zero exit status, execute the commands between **else** and **fi**.

select *variable* **in** *word1 word2 . . . wordn*
do
commands
done

Display a menu of numbered choices *word1* through *wordn* followed by a prompt (**#?** or **$PS3**). Execute *commands* for each menu selection, setting *variable* to each selection and **REPLY** to the response until a **break**, **exit**, or EOF is encountered.

select *variable*
do
commands
done

Display a menu of numbered choices for each positional parameter followed by a prompt (**#?** or **$PS3**). Execute *commands* for each menu selection, setting *variable* to each selection and **REPLY** to the response until a **break**, **exit**, or EOF is encountered.

until *command1*
do
commands
done

Execute *commands* until *command1* returns a zero exit status

while *command1*
do
commands
done

Execute *commands* while *command1* returns a zero exit status.

Special Commands:

:	null command; returns zero exit status
. *file*	read and execute commands in *file* in current environment
break	exit from current enclosing **for**, **select**, **until**, or **while** loop
break *n*	exit from *nth* enclosing **for**, **select**, **until**, or **while** loop
cd *dir*	change directory to *dir*. If *dir* not specified, change directory to **$HOME**.
cd *dir1 dir2*	change to directory where *dir1* in current pathname is substituted with *dir2*
cd –	change directory to the previous directory
echo *args*	display arguments

eval *commands*

read and execute commands

exec *I/O-redirection-command*

perform I/O redirection on file descriptors

exec *command*

replace current process with *command*

exit	exit with exit status of last command. If given at command prompt, terminate login shell.
exit *n*	exit from current program with exit status *n*
export	display a list of exported variables

export *var=value*

set *var* to *value* and export

export *vars*	export *vars*
false	return a non-zero exit status

fc –l[*options*] [*range*]

display *range* commands from history file according to *options*. If no *range* argument is given, display last 16 commands. Options are:

–n	do not display command numbers
–r	reverse the order

and *range* can be:

n1 [*n2*]	display list from command *n1* to command *n2*. If *n2* is not specified, display all commands from current command back to command *n1*.
–count	display last *count* commands
string	display all previous commands that matches *string*

fc [*options*] [*range*]

edit and re-execute range commands from the history file according to *options*. If no *range* argument is given, edit and re-execute last command. Options can be:

–e *editor*	use *editor* (default **FCEDIT** or **/bin/ed**)
–r	reverse the order

and *range* can be:

n1 n2	edit command *n1* to command *n2*
n	edit command *n*
–n	edit previous *nth* command
string	use all the previous commands back to command that matches *string*

fc –e – [*old=new*] [*command*]
edit and re-execute *command* where *old=new* specified to replace string *old* with *new* before executing. If no *command* given, use last command; *command* can be:

n	edit and re-execute command number *n*
–n	edit and re-execute last *nth* command
s tring	edit and re-execute most previous command that matches *string*

getopts *optsring name arguments*
parse *arguments*, using *optstring* as the list of valid options; save the option letter in *name*

getopts *optsring name*
parse positional parameters, using *optstring* as the list of valid options; save the option letter in *name*

newgrp change group-id to the default group-id

newgrp *gid*
change group id to *gid*

print [*options*] *arguments*
display *arguments* according to *options*

–	treat everything following – as an argument, even if it begins with –
–n	do not add a ending newline to the output
–p	redirect given arguments to a co-process
–r	ignore \ escape conventions
–R	ignore \ escape conventions; do not interpret – arguments as options
–s	redirect the given arguments to history file
–u*n*	redirect arguments to file descriptor *n*. If the file descriptor is greater than **2**, it must first be opened with **exec**. If *n* is not given, default file descriptor is **1 (stdout)**

print escape characters can be given with *arguments*:

\a	bell character
\b	backspace
\c	line without ending newline
\f	formfeed
\n	newline
\r	return
\t	tab
\v	vertical tab
****	backslash
\0*x*	8-bit character whose ASCII code is the 1-, 2-, or 3-digit octal number x

pwd display pathname of current directory

read [*options*] *variables*
read input into *variables* according to *options:*

–p	read input line from a co-process
–r	do not treat \ as line continuation char
–s	save copy of input line in history file
–u*n*	read input line from file descriptor *n*. If file descriptor is greater than **2**, it must first be opened with **exec**. If *n* not specified, default file descriptor is **0**.

read *name?prompt*
: display *prompt* and read the response into *name*

readonly display a list of readonly variables

readonly *var*
: set *var* to be readonly

readonly *var=value*
: set *var* to *value* and make it readonly

set	display a list of current variables and their values
set –o	display current option settings
set *args*	set positional parameters
set *–args*	set positional parameters even if they begin with –
set –s	sort positional parameters
set —	unset positional parameters
shift	shift positional parameters once left
shift *n*	shift positional parameters *n* times left

test *expression*
: evaluate *expression*

time *command*
: display elapsed, user, system time spent for *command*

times display the total user and system time for the current Korn shell and its child processes

trap *commands signals*
: execute *commands* when *signals* are received

trap "" *signals*
: ignore *signals*

trap *signals*, **trap** *–signals*
: reset traps to their default values

trap *commands* **0**, **trap** *commands* **EXIT**
: execute *commands* on exit

trap display a list of current traps

trap *commands* **DEBUG**
: execute *commands* after each command is executed

trap *commands* **ERR**
: if **errexit** (**–e**) option is enabled, then execute *commands* after commands that have a non-zero exit status

true	return a non-zero exit status
typeset	display a list of current variables and their values

ulimit [*options*] *n*
: set a resource limit to *n*. If *n* is not given, the specified resource limit is displayed. If no *option* is given, the file size limit (**–f**) is displayed; *options* can be:

–a	displays all current resource limits
–c *n*	set core dump size limit to *n* 512-byte blocks
–d *n*	set the data area size limit to *n* kilobytes
–f *n*	set child process file write limit to *n* blocks (default)
–m *n*	set physical memory size limit to *n* kilobytes
–s *n*	set stack area size limit to *n* kilobytes
–t *n*	set process time limit to *n* seconds
umask	display current value of file creation mask

umask *mask*
: set default file creation mask to *mask*

unset *var* remove definition of *var*

whence *name*
display information about *name*

whence –v *name*
display more information about *name*

Function Commands:

function *name* { *commands* **;** }
define a function *name*

return return from a function

return *n* return from a function; pass back return value of *n*

typeset –f display a list of functions and their definitions

typeset +f display a list of function names only

typeset –fu display a list of autoloading functions

typeset –fu *name*
make function *name* autoloading

typeset –fx display a list of exported functions

typeset –fx *name*
export function *name*

typeset –ft *name*
display function commands and arguments as they are executed

unset –f *name*
remove function *name*

Miscellaneous:

anything following a # to the end of the current line is treated as a comment and ignored

#!interpreter if the first line of a script starts with this, then the script is run by the specified interpreter

rsh the restricted shell is equivalent to **ksh**, except that changing directories, setting value of **ENV**, **PATH**, or **SHELL** variables, specifying path or command names containing /, or redirecting output of a command with >, >|, <>, or >> are not allowed

Files:

$HOME/.profile
contains local environment settings, such as search path, execution options, local variables, aliases, and more. At login time, it is read in and executed after **/etc/profile** file.

$HOME/.sh_history
contains previously executed commands

$ENV contains name of file that has aliases, function, options, variables, and other environment settings that are to be available to subshells

/etc/profile contains system-wide environment settings, such as a basic search path, a default **TERM** variable, the system **umask** value, and more (system dependent). If existent, it is read in and executed at login time before **$HOME/.profile** file.

/etc/suid_profile
contains local and system environment settings for privileged mode (system dependent)

layers - Layer Multiplexor (MISC)

$ layers [*options*] [*program*]

Description:

The **layers** command manages windows on windowing terminals.

Options:

–d	display sizes of the text, data, and bss portions of firmware patch on standard error (if downloaded)
–D	display debugging messages on standard error
–f *file*	start with initial configuration specified in *file*. Each line in *file* contains layer size and position: *x-origin y-origin x-corner y-corner commands*
–m *max*	set max size for data part of **xt** packet (**32–252**)
–p	display downloading protocol statistics on **stderr** (if a firmware patch has been downloaded)
–s	display protocol statistics on **stderr**
–t	enable **xt** driver packet tracing
program	specifies the file that contains the firmware patch that is downloaded before layers are created

Examples:

\# Invoke **layers** and initialize from **.layersrc**

$ layers .layersrc

ld - Link Editor for Object Files (PROG, BSD)

$ ld [*options*] *files*

$ /usr/ucb/ld [*options*] *files*

Description:

The **ld** command combines multiple object files, performs relocation, resolves external symbols, and supports symbol table information.

Options:

–a	create absolute file (static mode only, not with **–r**)
–A *sfile*	load incrementally using symbol table from *sfile* (**BSD**)
–Bdynamic	link with **lib***x***.so** first (see **–l***x* option)
–Bstatic	link with **lib***x***.a** first (see **–l***x* option)
–Bsymbolic	perform symbolic bind (in dynamic mode only)
–dn	use static linking
–dy	use dynamic linking (default)
–D *n*	pad to set data segment length to hexadecimal *n* (**BSD**)
–e *s*	set default entry point address to symbol *s*
–f *k*	set default fill pattern to constant *k*
–G	produce shared object instead of dynamic link
–h *name*	use *name* as dynamic link name
–I *name*	use name as interpreter for program header
–l*x*	search library **lib***x***.so** or **lib***x***.a**
–l*str*	search **lib***str***.a** in **–L** *dir*, then **/lib**, **/usr/lib**, **/usr/local** (**BSD**)
–L *dir*	search in *dir* before the standard directories

–m	display a memory map or listing of i/o sections
–M *map*	use *map* as link directives (static mode only)
–M	display names of files to be loaded (**BSD**)
–n	make text segment read-only and shared (**BSD**)
–N	do not make text segment read-only or shared (**BSD**)
–o *file*	put output in *file* (default **a.out**)
–Qn	suppress tool id information
–Qy	put tool id in information in output (default)
–r	generate relocatable output
–s	strip the symbol table and line number entries
–S	strip symbol table except local and global symbols (**BSD**)
–t	suppress multiply-defined symbol warnings
–t	display each file name as it is processed (**BSD**)
–T *n*	set text segment origin to hex *n* (default origin **0**) (**BSD**)
–u *s*	enter *s* as an undefined symbol in the symbol table
–V	display version information
–x	do not preserve local symbols in symbol table (**BSD**)
–X	save local symbols except for ones starting with **L** (**BSD**)
–YP, *dirs*	use *dirs* instead of default directories for finding libraries (*dirs* contains colon-separated directories)
–y*s*	list files with symbol *s* (**BSD**)
–z	load process on demand (default) (**BSD**)
–z defs	force error on undefined symbol
–z nodefs	allow undefined symbols
–z text	force error if relocations against no-writable allocatable sections remain

ldd – List Dynamic Dependencies (PROG)

$ ldd [*options*] *file*

Description:

The **ldd** command displays pathnames of all shared objects associated with *file*.

Options:

–d	check all reference to data objects
–r	check references to both data objects and functions

Examples:

\# Display shared objects associated with **xlogchk**

$ ldd xlogchk

lex - Generate Programs for Simple Lexical Tasks (MISC)

$ lex [*options*] [*files*]

Description:

The **lex** command generates programs used for simple lexical analysis of text. The input files contain strings and expressions to be searched for, and C source to be executed when they are found.

Options:

–c	indicates C actions (default)

–n	do not display summary
–Qn	suppress tool id information (default)
–Qy	put tool id in information in output
–t	send the output to standard output instead of **lex.yy.c**
–v	display a summary of statistics
–V	display version information
files	read standard input if no *files* are specified

line - Read One Line (MISC)

$ line

Description:

The **line** command copies a line read from **stdin** to **stdout.**

lint - Check C Programs (PROG)

$ lint [*options*] *files*

Description:

The **lint** command checks C source code in *files* for bugs, non-portability, type usage, and inefficient usage. Files with names ending in **.c** are interpreted as C source files. Files with names ending in **.ln** are interpreted as **lint** output files.

Options:

Most **cc** command-line options are also recognized.

–a	suppress warnings about assigning long values
–b	suppress warnings about unreachable **break**'s
–c	produce a **.ln** file for every **.c** file
–F	display pathnames of files
–h	do not apply heuristic tests
–I *dir*	search for **#include** files in *dir* first
–l*x*	include the additional lint library **llib-l***x***.ln**
–L *lib*	search lint libraries in *lib* first
–m	suppress complaints about external symbols that could be declared static
–n	suppress the standard/portable compatibility check
–o *lib*	create lint library **llib-l***lib***.ln** (not with **–c**)
–O	invoke the optimizer (recognized but ignored)
–p	check the portability against other C dialects
–R*file*	create a **.ln** file to *file* (for **cxref**)
–u	suppress warning messages about undefined functions and external variables
–v	suppress warnings about unused function args
–V	display version information
–W*file*	create a **.ln** file to *file* (for **cflow**)
–x	suppress warnings about unused external variables
–y	treat file as if **/*LINTLIBRARY*/** directive has been used

Examples:

Check **hello.c**; ignore warnings

$ lint –abmuvx hello.c

ln - Link Files (**FILE, BSD**)

$ ln [*options*] *file1 target*

$ **/usr/ucb/ln** [**–s**] *file1 file2*

$ **/usr/ucb/ln** [**–s**] *files directory*

Description:

The **ln** command links *file1* to *target*. If the target is not writable, invoker is prompted for a response. Unless **–s** is used, links may not span file systems or refer to directories.

Options:

–f	force link; do not display warning messages
–n	do not overwrite if the linkname is an existing file
–s	create a symbolic link (default hard link)

Examples:

Create a symbolic link between **ckque** and **/usr/local/bin**

$ ln –s ckque /usr/local/bin

logger - Make Entries in System Log (**BSD**)

$ /usr/ucb/logger [*options*] [*message*]

Description:

The **logger** command creates system log entries.

Options:

–f *file*	log file
–i	log process id of logger process with each line
–p *prior*	enter message with specified priority; priority may be number or *facility.level* (default **user.notice**)
–t *tag*	mark every line in the log with *tag*
message	log *message*

login - Log Onto System (**MISC**)

$ login [*user*] [*variable=value* **. . .**]]

Description:

The **login** command allows a user to log onto the system. If *user* is not given, the user is prompted for one. If **login** is invoked as a command, the **exec** command must precede it. The environment can also be initialized with optional command-line variable assignments.

logname - Display Login Name (**MISC**)

$ logname

Description:

The **logname** command shows the value of **LOGNAME**.

lorder - Find Ordering Relation for Object Library (**PROG**)

$ lorder *files*

Description:

The **lorder** command generates a list of pairs of object file names from the given archive file names. The first file name refers to external identifiers in the second file.

Examples:

\# Build a new library from object files

$ ls *.o | lorder | tsort | ar –cr lib.a

lp - Send Print-Request to a Printer (**PRINT**)

$ lp [*options*] *files*

$ lp –i *ID* [*options*]

Description:

The **lp** command sends *files* to be printed by a printer. It returns an id associated with the print request.

Options:

–c — copy *files* to spooler instead of linking. If not given, do not modify or remove *files* before printing is completed.

–d*dest* — send print request to printer or printer class *dest*. If *dest* is a class, printing will be done on first available printer in that class. If –**d***dest* is not given, **$LPDEST** or the system default is used.

–f *form-name* [**–d any**] — print request on *form-name*. If **–d any** used, printer with *form-name* mounted is used.

–H *command* — print request according to *command*:

hold	suspend request until further notice
immediate	print request next
resume	resume printing of suspended request

–i *ID* — change options for request associated with *ID*

–m — send mail when finished printing

–n*n* — print *n* copies (default **1**)

–o*option* — specify a printer or class dependent option. Multiple **–o** arguments can be given.

cpi=*scale*	print request according to *scale* character pitch; *scale* can be a decimal number followed by **i** (inches), **c** (centimeters), **pica**, **elite**, or **compressed** (not with **–f**)
length=*scale*	print request according to *scale* length; *scale* can be a decimal number followed by **i** (inches) or **c** (cent.)
lpi=*scale*	print request according to *scale* line pitch; *scale* can be a decimal number followed by **i** (inches) or **c** (cent.)
nobanner	do not print a banner page
nofilebreak	do not insert formfeed between files
stty=*options*	list of valid **stty** options
width=*scale*	print request according to *scale* width; *scale* can be a decimal number followed by **i** (inches) or **c** (cent.)

–s	suppress diagnostic messages
–S *charset* [**–d any**]	print request with given charset or print-wheel. If **–d any** given, then request is printed on any printer with *charset* or *print-wheel* mounted.
–t*string*	print *string* on banner page of output
–T *content-type* [**–r**]	print request on printer that supports *content-type*. If **–r** given, do not use a filter.
–w	notify user when finished printing; send mail if user not logged on
–y *modes*	print request according to *modes*
files	read standard input if – or no *files* specified

Variables:

LPDEST	contains the name of the printer or printer class

Examples:

\# Print two copies of **file**

$ lp –n2 file

\# Print *.c on printer **lpqms** and send **mail** when finished

$ lp –dlpqrms *.c

lpq - Report Status of Print Jobs (BSD)

$ **/usr/ucb/lpq** [*options*] [*jobs*] [*users*]

Description:

The **lpq** command checks the status of print jobs.

Options:

–l	display information about files in *jobs*
–P	show status of queue for default printer or **$PRINTER**
–P*printer*	report status of print queue for *printer*
+	show queue status until it is empty
+*n*	sleep *n* seconds before displaying queue status
jobs	show status of specified jobs only
users	report status for jobs associated with *users* only

Variables:

PRINTER	contains name of default printer

lpr - Send Output to Line Printer Spooler (BSD)

$ **/usr/ucb/lpr** [*options*] [*files*]

Description:

The **lpr** command sends *files* to the print queue.

Options+

–c	input files contain data produced by **cifplot**
–C*str*	print *str* instead of default system name on banner page
–d	input files contain data produced by **tex**
–f	interpret first character of each line as Fortran carriage control
–g	input files contain data produced by plot

–h	do not print burst page
–i*n*	indent output *n* spaces (default **8** if *n* not specified)
–J*str*	print *str* instead of default file name on banner page
–l	print control characters and suppress page breaks
–m	send mail when printing has completed
–n	input files contain data produced by **ditroff**
–p	format files using **pr**
–P	send output to default printer or **$PRINTER** if set
–P*ptr*	send output to printer *ptr*
–r	remove files after spooling or printing
–s	create symbolic links to spool directory instead of copying
–t	input files contain data produced by **troff**
–T*title*	use *title* instead of file name for **pr** title
–v	input files contain raster image
–w*n*	set page width to *n* for **pr**
–#n	print *n* copies of files
–nfont	mount specified *font* on position *n* (**1**, **2**, **3** or **4**)
files	read **stdin** if no *files* specified

lprm - Remove Job from Printer Spooler Queue (**BSD**)

$ **/usr/ucb/lprm** [*options*] [*jobs*] [*users*]

Description:

The **lprm** command removes all or specified *jobs* from the print queue.

Options:

–P	remove jobs from default printer or **$PRINTER** if set
–P*ptr*	remove jobs from printer *ptr*
–	remove all jobs belonging to *users;* if run by the super-user, all jobs removed
jobs	remove specified jobs only

lprof – Display Execution Profile Data (**PROG**)

$ lprof [*options*]

$ lprof –m *file*.**cnt** [–**T**] **–d** *destfile***cnt**

Description:

The **lprof** command displays program execution characteristics on a line by line basis. It can also be used to merge execution profile files.

Options:

–c*file*	use *file* **.cnt** instead of *prog*.**cnt** as input profile file
–I *dir*	search for source or header files in *dir* along with the standard search path
–m *file1*.**cnt** *file2*.**cnt** . . . *filen*.**cnt** **–d** *destfile*.**cnt**	merge data files *file1*.**cnt** through *filen*.**cnt** and put results in *destfile*.**cnt**
–o *prog*	use *prog* instead of name used when profile file created
–p	display line-numbered listing with execution count
–r *files*	display only the given source files (only with **–p**)

–s display summary information of percentage of code executed per function
–T do not check time stamps
–V display version information
–x precede lines not executed with a [**U**]

Variables:

PROFOPTS
contains a comma-separated list of options that control profiling, which can be:

dir=*dir* put data file in *dir* (default current directory)
file=*file* use *file* as name of data file in *dir*
merge=*option*
specify how to handle data files:
n overwrite data files after each execution (default)
y merge data files
msg=*option*
specify which messages to display:
n display only error messages
y data file name format
pid=*option* specify data file name format:
n do not include program PID in data file name (default)
y include program PID in data file name

Examples:

\# Display execution summary statistics for **hck**

$ lprof –s hck

lpstat - Display Printer Status Information (PRINT)

$ lpstat [*options*]

Description:

The **lpstat** command displays information about the system printer services. The status of the invokers print requests is displayed if no options are given.

Options:

–a[*list*] display the acceptance status of all or the given destinations (printers or printer classes)
–c[*list*] display the members of all or the given classes
–d display the default destination printer
–f [*list*] verify that given or all forms are recognized
–f [*list*] **–l** display a description for all or given forms
–o[*list*] display the status of all or the given print requests (printers, printer classes, or print request ids)
–p[*list*] display the status of all or the given printers
–p[*list*] **–D** display a brief description for all or given printers
–p [*list*] **–l** display full description for all or given printers
–r display the status of the **lp** request scheduler
–R display position of job in queue
–s display the status summary (same as **–rdcu**)

–S [*list*] **–l**	verify that all or given character sets are recognized. If **–l** given, display a list or printers that can handle print wheel or character set.
–t	display all status information
–u[*list*]	display the status of all or given users print requests. The user list can be given as: *user*, *system*!*user*, *system*!**all**, **all**!*user*, **all**!**all**, **all**
–v[*list*]	display the device pathnames for all or the given printers
list	items separated by commas or enclosed in quotes and separated by one or more spaces

Examples:

\# Display the status for printers **lpt1**, **lpt2**, and **lpt3**

$ lpstat –ulpt1,lpt2,lpt3

\# Display the status of print requests for **xp2**

$ lpstat –oxp2

\# Display all status information

$ lpstat –t

lptest - Generate Lineprinter Ripple Pattern (PRINT, BSD)

$ **lptest** [*length*[*n*]]

$ **/usr/ucb/lptest** [*length*[*n*]]

Description:

The **lptest** command displays a ripple test pattern.

Options:

length	set output line length to *n* (default **79**)
n	generate *n* output lines (default **200**)

ls - List Contents of Directory (FILE, BSD)

$ ls [*options*] [*directories* | *files*]

$ /usr/ucb/ls [*options*] [*directories* | *files*]

Description:

The **ls** command lists the contents of *directories* or *files*. If no *directories* or *files* given, list contents of the current directory.

Options:

–a	list all entries, including those that begin with **.**
–A	list all entries except those that begin with **.** and **..** (**BSD**)
–b	display non-graphic characters in octal **\nnn** format
–c	sort by last modification time of inode (with **–l**, **–t**)
–C	list in multi-column format with entries sorted down
–d	if an argument is a directory, list the name only
–f	interpret each argument as a directory (disables **–l**, **–r**, **–s**, **–t** and enables **–a**)
–F	put / after directories, * after executables, @ after symbolic links
–g	same as **–l**, except that owner is not displayed
–g	include group ownership in long format (**BSD**)
–i	display inode number in the first column
–l	list in long format; display mode, number of links, owner, group, byte size, and last modification time

–L	list file or directory referenced by the symbolic link (**BSD**)
–m	stream output; list files across separated with ,'s
–n	same as **–l**, except that the owner and group ID's are displayed instead of the character string
–o	same as **–l**, except that the group is not displayed
–p	put / after directories
–q	display non-printable characters as **?**
–r	reverse order of the sort
–R	recursively list subdirectories
–s	display entry size in blocks
–t	sort by modification time
–u	sort by last access time (with **–l** or **–t**)
–x	list in multi-column format
–1	display one entry per line

Variables:

COLUMNS
contains the line length (default **80**)

Examples:

\# List contents of **/usr** with its subdirectories in long format

$ ls –lR /usr

\# List in modification order with / after directories

$ ls –lup

m4 - Macro Processor (**PROG**)

$ m4 [*options*] [*files*]

Description:

The **m4** command preprocesses files that contain C or other language source code.

Options:

–B *n*	change push-back and argument collection buffer sizes to *n* (default **4096**)
–D*var=y*	define *var* to *y* or null if =*y* not specified
–e	process interactively
–H*n*	change hash array size to *n* (default **199**)
–s	enable line sync output for C preprocessor
–S*n*	change call stack size to *n* (default **100**)
–T*n*	change token buffer size to *n* (default **512**)
–U*var*	undefine *var*
files	read standard input if *files* is – or no *files* specified

mail - Send/Read Mail (**MISC**)

$ mail [*options*]
$ mail [*options*] *users*

Description:

The **mail** command reads mail messages or sends mail messages to *users*. Mail messages are read from standard input up to end of file (**^D**), or until a line with just a period is entered.

Read Mail Options:

–e	do not display mail messages; return exit code **0** if invoker has mail, otherwise return exit code **1**
–f*file*	use *file* instead of default mail file (default **mbox**)
–h	display window of headers followed by the **?** prompt
–p	display all mail messages without prompts
–P	display all mail messages and headers
–q	exit from **mail** after interrupts
–r	display mail messages in first-in first-out order

Send Mail Options:

–m *type*	add **Message-type:** *type* to message header
–t	include the **To:** line with the recipients
–T *file*	display how system mailsurr *file* is parsed
–w	send mail; do not wait for completion of remote transfer
–x*n*	set debugging level to *n*
users	for remote system users, UUCP-style (*system!user*), and/or Domain-style (*user@system*) addressing may be used (see system administrator)

Forwarding Mail:

–F*users*	forward incoming mail messages to *users.* The mailbox must be empty. An **Auto-Forwarded-From:** line is added to the forwarded message.
–F ""	remove mail forwarding
–F | *cmd*	pipe mail messages to *cmd*. Keywords are substituted before command is executed:

%c	value of **Content-Type:** header
%R	return path of the originator
%S	value of **Subject:** header

Read Mail Commands:

a	display mail messages that arrive during current session
d, **dp**	delete mail message and go on to next mail message
d *n*	delete mail messsage *n*
dq	delete mail message and exit from **mail**
h	display window of headers around current message
h *n*	display the header for mail message *n*
h a	display headers for all mail messages in *mailfile*
h d	display headers for mail messages scheduled for deletion
m *users*	send the mail message to the specified *users*
n	go to the next mail message
p	display the current mail message
q, **^D**	put undeleted mail in *maifile* and exit from **mail**
r	reply to sender, then delete the mail message
r *users*	reply to sender and *users*, then delete mail message
s, **y**	save mail message in **mbox**
s *files*	save mail message in *files*
u [*n*]	undelete the current or specified mail message
w	save mail message without top header in **mbox**
w *files*	save mail message without the top header in *files*
x	put all mail messages in *mailfile* and exit **mail**

+,<Return>	go to next mail message
–	display the previous mail message
?	display the command summary
!*cmd*	escape to shell and execute *cmd*
n	display mail message *n*

Delivery Notification:

Transport-Options: [*options*] ,
Default-Options: [*options*] ,
>To: *recipient* [*options*]

specify delivery notification where *options* may be:

/delivery	inform sender of successful deliveries
/ignore	do not inform sender of unsuccessful deliveries
/nodelivery	do not inform sender of successful deliveries
/report	same as **/return**, except original message not returned
/return	inform sender if mail delivery fails and return message (default)

Files:

$HOME/dead.letter
contains unmailable messages

$HOME/mbox
contains saved mail messages

/var/mail/*user*
contains incoming mail messages (*mailfile*)

Examples:

Display mail headers only
$ mail –h

Send **rep.out** to **root@mach**
$ cat rep.out | mail root@mach

mailalias – Display Mail Alias Names (MISC)

$ mailalias [*options*] *names*

Description:

The **mailalias** command displays a list of addresses associated with the alias *name*. The alias files **/var/mail/***name*, **$HOME/lib/***names*, **/etc/mail/namefiles** are searched in order for a match. If an alias file is a directory, then a file *name* in that directory is also checked.

Options:

–s	do not include name in output
–v	display debugging information on **stdout**

Examples:

Display alias for **allusers**
$ mailalias allusers

mailx

mailx - Interactive Mail Processing System (MISC)

$ mailx [*options*] [*names*]

Description:

The **mailx** command provides an interactive interface for sending, receiving, and manipulating mail messages. The Basic Networking Utilities must be installed for some of the remote features to work. Incoming mail is stored in the primary mail file, called the **mailbox**. As mail is read, it is moved to the secondary mail file (unless specific action taken), called the **mbox**.

Read Mail Options:

–e	check for mail; return **0** if there is mail to read
–f [*file*]	read mail messages from *file* instead of **mailbox**. If no *file* is given, use **mbox**.
–H	display mail header summary only
–I	include newsgroup and article-id header in output
–n	do not initialize from **/etc/mailx.rc** file
–N	do not display the initial mail header summary
–T *file*	save message-id and article-id header lines in *file*
–u *user*	read given user's mailbox (if permissions allow)
–V	display version information

Send Mail Options:

–d	enable debugging output
–F	save the mail message in a file named after the first recipient; overrides **record** (see **Variables**)
–h *n*	specify the number of network hops made so far
–i	ignore interrupts (see **ignore**)
–n	do not initialize from **/etc/mailx.rc** file
–r *addr*	pass *addr* to network delivery software
–s *string*	set the **Subject** field to *string*
–U	convert **uucp** style addresses to internet style addresses; overrides **conv** (see **addsopt**)
–V	display version information

Commands:

format: [*command*] [*message-list*] [*arguments*]

a *alias names*, **g** *alias names*
: create an *alias* for *names*; (*names* are substituted for *alias* when used as a mail recipient)

alt *names* create list of alternate names to not receive responses

cd [*dir*], **ch** [*dir*]
: change working directory to *dir* (default **$HOME**)

c [*file*], **c** [*msgs*] *file*
: copy specified mail messages to *file* without marking them as saved

C [*msgs*] save specified mail messages in file named after mail sender (do not mark messages as saved)

d [*msglist*] delete specified mail messages.

di [*headers*], **ig** [*headers*]
: do not include *headers* when displaying messages

dp [*msglist*], **dt** [*msglist*]
: delete specified mail messages from **mailbox** and display next message

e *strings* echo *strings*
e [*msglist*] edit the specified mail messages using the editor from **EDITOR** (default **ed**)
ex exit from **mailx** without changing **mailbox**; no mail messages saved in **mbox**
f [*file*], **fold** [*file*]
exit from current mail message file and read in *file*. If *file* is not given, the current **mailbox** is used. Files can also be:

%	current **mailbox**
%*user*	user **mailbox** for *user*
#	previous file
&	current **mbox**

folders display name of files in directory from **folder**
f [*message*] respond to specified mail message. Save a copy of response in file named after mail sender.
F [*msglist*] repond to first mail message in *msglist*. Use subject line from original mail message for response. Save a copy of response in a file named after sender.
f [*msglist*] display header summary for the specified messages
h [*message*] display page of headers which includes *message*. Number of headers per page controlled by **screen**.
help display a command summary
ho [*msglist*], **pre** [*msglist*]
save specified mail messages in *mailbox*
if *send* | *read*
mail-cmds1
else
mail-cmds2
endiff execute *mail-cmds1* if in send mode, and execute *mail-cmds2* if in receive mode
ignore *headers*, **discard** *headers*
do not display *headers*
l display list of available commands
m *users* send mail message to *users*
mb [*msglist*]
save specified messages in standard **mbox**
n [*msglist*], **n** [*message*]
go to next mail message in *msglist* or one that matches *message*
p [*msglist*] [*cmd*] | [*msglist*] [*cmd*]
pipe specified mail messages through *cmd*
pre [*msglist*], **ho** [*msglist*]
save specified mail messages in **mailbox**
p [*msglist*] display specified mail messages. If **crt** is set, long messages are paged through **$PAGER**.
P [*msglist*] display specified mail messages
q exit from **mailx** and save read mail messages in **mbox** and unread mail messages in **mailbox**
r [*msglist*] reply to all specified mail messages
R [*msglist*] reply to author of each of the specified mail messages
s [*file*], **s** [*msglist*] *file*
save specified mail messages to *file*

S [*msglist*] save specified mail messages in file whose name is taken from author of first message (without network addressing)

set, **set** *var*, **set var=***string*, **set var=***number*
define variable *var* and set it to the given value. If no *var* is specified, display all defined variables and their values.

sh invoke an interactive shell

si [*msglist*] display size of the specified mail messages

so *file* read commands from *file*, return to command mode

to [*msglist*] display top lines of given mail messages (default **5**)

tou [*msglist*]
touch given mail messages. If any message in *msglist* not saved, place it in **mbox**, or **$MBOX**.

t [*msglist*] display specified mail messages. If **crt** is set, messages longer than **crt** are displayed through **$PAGER**.

T [*msglist*] display specified mail messages

u [*msglist*] restore specified mail messages that were deleted

un *vars* remove the definition of the specified variables

ve display version number and release date

v [*msglist*] edit mail messages using editor from **$VISUAL**

w [*msglist*] *file*
write the specified mail messages to *file*

x exit from **mailx** without changing **mailbox**; no mail messages saved in **mbox**

z + scroll the header display forward one screenfull

z – scroll the header display backward one screenfull

#string *string* is taken as comments and ignored

= display the message number

? display a command summary

!*cmd* escape to the shell and execute *cmd*

msglist single or multiple space-separated mail message id numbers. If no *msglist* specified, use the current message.

Mail Message Identifiers:

n message number *n*

. current mail message

^ first undeleted mail message

$ last mail message

* all mail messages

m–n range of mail message numbers

user all mail messages from *user*

/*string* all mail messages with *string* in **Subject** line

:*c* all type *c* mail messages, where *c* can be:

- **d** deleted mail messages
- **n** new mail messages
- **o** old mail messages
- **r** read mail messages
- **u** unread mail messages

Tilde Escapes:

The following tilde escape commands can only be entered from input mode or by preceding the command with a tilde escape character.

~A	put autograph string **Sign** into mail message
~a	put autograph string **sign** into mail message
~b *names*	add *names* to blind carbon copy (**Bcc:**) list
~c *names*	add *names* to carbon copy (**Cc:**) list
~d	read in **dead.letter** file
~e	invoke editor from **$EDITOR** on the partial message
~f [*msglist*]	forward specified mail messages
~h	prompt for **Subject**, **To**, **Cc**, and **Bcc** lists
~i *var*	put he value of variable *var* into the mail message
~m [*msglist*]	insert specified mail messages and shift right one tab stop (only when sending message while reading mail)
~p	print message being entered
~q	exit from input mode; save mail message in **dead.letter** (see **DEAD**)
~r *file*, **~~<** *file*	read specified file into the mail message
~s *string*	set **Subject** line to *string*
~t *users*	add the specified user names to the **To** list
~v	invoke the screen editor from **$VISUAL**
~w *file*	write partial mail message without headers to *file*
~x	exit from input mode
~| *cmd*	pipe mail message without headers through the given shell command. If *cmd* returns a successful exit status, output of *cmd* replaces mail message.
~!*cmd*	escape to shell and execute the specified command
~~< !*cmd*	read specified shell command into mail message
~.	terminate message input
~:*mail-cmd*, ~_*mail-cmd*	execute given mail command (only when sending a message while reading mail)
~?	display tilde escape summary

Variables:

[no]allnet	treat network names with identical login names the same (default **noallnet**)
[no]append	append messages to **mbox** (default **noappend**)
[no]askcc	prompt for the **Cc** list (default **noaskcc**)
[no]askbcc	prompt for **Bcc** list (default **noaskbcc**)
[no]autoprint	enable automatic displaying of messages after delete and undelete (default **noautoprint**)
[no]bang	enable special-casing of **!** (default **nobang**)
cmd=*cmd*	set default command for the pipe command
conv=internet	convert **uucp** addresses to internet style address
crt=*n*	pipe messages with more than *n* lines through the command specified by **$PAGER**
DEAD=*file*	save partial messages in *file* (default **dead.letter**)
[no]debug	enable verbose debugging; messages are not delivered (default **nodebug**)
[no]dot	accept period on a line by itself as EOF (default **nodot**)

EDITOR=*cmd*
set editor command for **e**, **~e** to *cmd*(default **ed**)

escape=*c* set escape character for ~ to *c* (default ~)

folder=*dir* save mail messages to files in *dir*. If *dir* does not start with a /, **$HOME** is prepended to it. User specified files beginning with a **+** are expanded by prepending *dir* to it.

header enable displaying of header summary when entering **mailx** (default enabled)

[no]hold save all mail messages read in **mailbox** instead of in **mbox** (default **nohold**)

[no]ignore ignore interrupts while editing mail messages (default **noignore**)

[no]ignoreeof
ignore EOF while editing mail messages. The input must be terminated by a period on a line by itself or by **~.** command. (default **noignoreeof**)

keep truncate **mailbox** instead of removing (default disabled)

[no]keepsave
save messages that have been saved in other mailboxes instead of deleting (default **nokeepsave**)

LISTER=*cmd*
set command to use when listing contents of the folder directory (default **ls**)

MAILRC contains name of startup file (default **$HOME/.mailrc**)

MBOX=*file*
save read mail messages in *file* (default **$HOME/mbox**)

[no]metoo do not delete the invoker's name from recipient list (default **nometoo**)

onehop disable alteration of recipients addresses when responding

[no]outfolder
save outgoing messages in files in **folder** unless the pathname is absolute (default **nooutfolder**)

[no]page used with **pi** to insert a form feed after each mail message (default **nopage**)

PAGER=*cmd*
use *cmd* as the filter for paging output (default **pg**)

prompt=*string*
set command mode prompt to *string* (default **?**)

[no]quiet do not display the opening message and version number when entering **mailx** (default **noquiet**)

record=*file* save all outgoing mail messages in *file* (default disabled)

save save mail messages in **dead.letter** on interrupt or error (default enabled)

screen=*n* set number of lines for **h** command to *n*

sendmail=*cmd*
use *cmd* for delivering mail messages (default **/bin/rmail**)

[no]sendwait
wait for background mail to finish before proceeding (default **nosendwait**)

SHELL=*cmd*
use *cmd* for shell escapes (default **sh**)

showto use recipient's name instead of the author's name when displaying header summaries
sign=*string* use *string* for the **~a** autograph command (no default)
Sign=*string* use *string* for the **~A** command (no default)
toplines=*n* set number of header lines to display with **t** command to *n*
VISUAL=*cmd*
use *cmd* as screen editor (default **vi**)

Files:

$HOME/.mailrc
contains **mailx** startup command

$HOME/mbox
secondary mail message storage file

/etc/mailx/mailx.rc
contains **mailx** startup commands

Examples:

Display the mail header summaries only
$ mailx –H

Send **file1** to **user** and set the subject field to "**Here is file1**"
$ cat file1 | mailx –s "Here is file1" user

Read mail messages from **savebox**
$ mailx –f savebox

make - Maintain Groups of Programs (PROG)

$ make [*options*] [*files*]

Description:

The **make** command updates *files* according to commands from the description file. Target files are only updated if the dependents are newer than target. Missing files are interpreted as out of date.

Options:

–e make environment variables override assignments
–f *mfile* use *mfile* as the description file. If no **–f** option is specified, use **makefile**, **Makefile**, **s.makefile**, or **s.Makefile**. If *makefile* is **–**, use standard input.
–i ignore error codes returned by invoked commands (see also **.IGNORE**)
–k continue on to next entry that is not dependent on current entry on error
–m display the memory map showing text, data and stack
–n display, but do not execute commands. Lines beginning with @ are also displayed.
–p display macro definitions and target descriptions
–q return true if target is up to date, otherwise return false
–r do not use the built-in rules
–s do not display commands before executing them
–t touch target files without executing commands

Target Names:

These options are specified when present in the **Makefile**.

.DEFAULT
: commands associated with this target are used when a file must be made with no explicit commands or built-in rules

.IGNORE
: ignore error codes returned by invoked command

.PRECIOUS
: dependents associated with this target are not removed on interrupt or quit

.SILENT do not display commands before executing them

.SUFFIXES contains additional suffixes. If none are given, suffix list is cleared.

Command Format:

The description file (**Makefile**) contains entries that specify targets and dependencies. The first line of an entry contains blank-separated targets, terminated with a **:**, followed by a list of dependencies. All following lines beginning with a tab are interpreted as shell commands and used to update the targets. The update command lines are continued onto the next line if they end with ****. The command lines can also be prefixed by:

–	ignore errors
@	don't display the command
–@, @–	ignore errors and don't display the command
#	interpret as comments and ignore

Macros:

Macro entries have the format *macro* = *value* and are used like variables in shell scripts. If **D** or **F** are appended to the first four macros, it is interpreted as the directory part (**D**), or the file part (**F**). This is equivalent to the **dirname** or **basename** of the macro.

$*	file name of current dependent without suffix
$@	full target name of current target
$<	module name which is out of date
$%	archive library member file name
$?	list of prerequisites that are out of date
macro=value	declare a macro and set its value
$(*macro*)	value of *macro*

Variables:

CFLAGS	contains default **cc** options
MAKEFLAGS	contains current command line options
YFLAGS	contains default **yacc** options

Examples:

\# Rules to make **hello** from **a.c**, and **b.c**

```
hello:      a.o b.o
            cc  a.o b.o $CFLAGS –o hello
a.o b.o:    a.c b.c
            cc –c *.c
```

makey - Generate Encryption Key (MISC)

$ **/usr/lib/makekey**

Description:
The **makey** command generates an encryption key by from **stdin**.

man - Display Entries from Manual (MISC, BSD)

$ **/usr/ucb/man** [–] [**–M** *path*] [*section*] *titles*
$ **/usr/ucb/man –f** *files*
$ **/usr/ucb/man –k** *keywords*

Description:
The **man** command displays man pages, or a one line synopsis for man pages whose description contains any keywords.

Options:

–f *files*	print one-line synopsis for sections related to *files*
–k *keywords*	display one-line synopsis for sections containing *keywords*
–M *path*	search for entries in **$path** or **$MANPATH** if set
–t	generate **troff** output for a raster device
–	pipe output through **more –s** (default for terminals)
section	search for man pages in *section*, which can be a number, or **local**, **new**, **old**, or **public**.

mcs – Manipulate Comment Section of Object Files (PROG)

$ **mcs** [*options*] *file*

Description:
The **mcs** command manipulates the comment section of an object file.

Options:

–a *string*	append *string* to comment section
–c	compress comment section
–d	delete comment section
–n *section*	access given *section* (default **.comment**)
–p	display comment section
–V	display version information

Example:
\# Display the comment section of **/bin/rnews**
$ mcs –p /bin/rnews

mesg - Permit/Deny Messages (MISC)

$ **mesg** [*options*]

Description:
The **mesg** command controls messages made via **write**. If no *options* are given, current **mesg** state is displayed.

Options:

–n	do not allow messages
–y	permit messages

Example:
\# Do not allow messages
$ mesg –n

mkdir - Create Directory (**FILE**)

$ mkdir [*options*] *directories*

Description:

The **mkdir** command creates *directories* with the user and group ID's set to the invokers real user and group ID.

Options:

–m *mode*	specify mode for new directory
–p	create non-existing parent directories if needed

Examples:

\# Create **/tmp/test/p012** and all subdirectories

$ mkdir –p /tmp/test/p012

mkmsgs - Create Message Files from Strings (**MISC**)

$ mkmsgs [*options*] *stringfile msgfile*

Description:

The **mkmsgs** command creates a file of text strings for use with the text retrieval tools.

Options:

–i *locale*	put *msgfile* in **/usr/lib/locale/***locale***/LC_MESSAGES**
–o	overwrite msgfile

Examples:

\# Create message file from **error.str**

$ mkmsgs error.str EX

mkstr - Create Error Message File from C Programs (**BSD**)

$ **/usr/ucb/mkstr** [–] *errorfile prefix files*

Description:

The **mkstr** command creates files of error messages. The error messages from *files* are placed in *errorfile* and the processed source files are put in *files* prefixed with *prefix*.

Options:

–	append error message to the end of *errorfile*

more - Display Files (**FILE, BSD**)

$ more [*options*] [–*n*] [+*n*] [+/*pattern*/] [*files*]

$ /usr/ucb/more [**–cdflsu**] [–*n*] [+*n*] [+/*pattern*/] [*files*]

Description:

The **more** command displays *files* one screenful at a time.

Options:

–c	redraw each page instead of scrolling
–d	display long prompt after each page and on error
–f	count by newlines instead of by screen lines
–l	do not treat **^L** (formfeed) as special character
–r	display control characters as **^***c*

–s	truncate multiple blank lines into one line
–u	suppress terminal underlining or stand-out mode
–w	prompt before exiting
–n	set window size to *n* lines (default from **stty**)
+n	start displaying at line *n*
+/pattern/	start two lines before line containing *pattern*

Commands:

Commands are entered between displays. If not specified, the default for *n* is **1**.

[*n*]**b**, [*n*]**B**	go back *n* screens
[*n*]**d**, [*n*]<Space>	display *n* more lines (default **11**)
^D	display **11** more lines
*n***^D**	set scroll size to *n* lines
[*n*]**f**	skip *n* screens
h	display information about **more** commands
q, **Q**	exit from **more**
[*n*]**s**	skip *n* lines
v	invoke **vi** at the current line
*n***z**	set window size to *n* lines
<Space>,**z**	display another screen
=	display current line number
n/expression	search for *nth* occurrence of *expression*
*n***n**	search for *nth* occurrence of last expression entered
:f	display the current file name and line number
*n***:n**	go to *nth* next file given on the command line
*n***:p**	go to *nth* previous file given on the command line
:q, **:Q**	same as **q**
.	repeat the previous command
!*cmd*	escape to the shell and execute *cmd*

Examples:

\# Display **rep.out**; truncate multiple blank lines

$ more –s rep.out

\# Display **Articles** with a long prompt

$ more –d Articles

mv - Link Files (**FILE**)

$ mv[*options*] *file1 file2*

$ mv [*options*] *files directory*

$ mv [*options*] *directory1 directory2*

Description:

The **mv** command moves *file1* to *file2*, or *files* to *directory*. The **mv** command also moves *directory1* to *directory2* if they both have the same parent directory. If the target is not writable, the invoker is prompted for a response.

Options:

–f	force the move; do not display a warning message
–i	prompt for confirmation before overwriting

Example:

\# Move **file1**, **file2**, and **file3** to **/var/spool/uucppublic**

$ mv file[1–3] /var/spool/uucppublic

nawk

nawk - Pattern Scanning and Processing Language (**MISC**)

$ nawk [*options*] ['*program*'] [*files*]

Description:

The **nawk** command performs actions for lines in *files* that match *patterns* specified in *program*. Each input line is made up of fields separated by regular expression *regexp*.

Options:

–f *file*	get patterns from *file* instead of *program*
–F*c*	separate fields with character *c* (default whitespace)
–v *var=value*	assign *value* to variable *var* (multiple **–v**'s can be given)
files	read **stdin** if *files* is – or no *files* are specified

Program Structure:

See **AWK**

Operators: (see also **AWK**)

(*exp*)	grouping
exp1 **?** *exp2* **:** *exp3*	conditional

Variables:

ARGC	command-line argument count
ARGV	command-line argument array
FILENAME	input file currently being read
FNR	record number of current record in current file
FS	input field separator (default blank and tab)
NF	number of fields in the current record
NR	current record number
OFMT	output format for numbers (default **%g**)
OFS	output field separator (default blank)
ORS	output record separator (default newline)
RS	input record separator (default newline)
SUBSEP	separates multiple subscripts
0	entire current input record
n	*nth* input field of current record

Functions:

atan2(*exp1*,*exp2*)	return arctangent of *exp1/exp2*
close(*file*)	close the specified file or pipe
cos(*exp*)	return cosine of *exp*
exp(*exp*)	exponential of *exp*
getline()	set next input record to **$0**
getline < *file*	set **$0** to next record from *file*
getline *var*	set *var* to next input record
getline *var* < *file*	set *var* to next input record from *file*
gsub(*regexp*, *string1*, *string2*)	substitute *string1* for all instances of *regexp* in *string2*. If *string2* not specified, use the current record **$0**.

index(*s1*,*s2*)
return position of string *s1* in string *s2*

int(*expr*) return integer value of *expr*

length(*s1*) return length of string *s1*

log(*exp*) return natural logarithm of *exp*

match(*string*, *regexp*)
return position in *string* where *regexp* occurs. If not found, return **0**. **RSTART** is set to the starting position, and **RLENGTH** is set to length of *string*.

rand(*n*) return random number between 0 and 1

sin(*exp*) return sine of *exp* radions

split(*s1*,*a*) split *s1* into *a*[**1**]–*a*[*n*] using **$FC**

split(*s1*,*a*,*c*)split *s1* into *a*[**1**]–*a*[*n*] using *c*

sprintf(*fmt*,*expr*)
format *expr* according to the **printf** format *fmt*

sqrt(*exp*) return square root of *exp*

srand(*expr*)set seed value for **rand** to *expr*

srand() set seed value for **rand** to time of day

system(*cmd*)
return exit value from *cmd*

sub(*regexp*, *string1*, *string2*)
substitute *string1* for first instance of *regexp* in *string2*. If *string2* not given, use current record **$0**.

substr(*s*,*x*) return suffix of string *s* starting at *x*

substr(*s*,*x*,*n*)
return *n*-character substring of *s* starting at *x*

cmd | **getline**
pipe output of *cmd* into **getline**. Successive calls to **getline** return the next line of output from *cmd*.

function *name*(*args*,...) {*statements*}

func *name*(*args*,...) {*statements*}
specify a function *name* that executes *statements*. Function calls can be nested and recursive.

Examples:

Display fields of **file** separated with sequences of **a**

$ nawk '{FS = "a*" ; print $1, $3}' file

Display the lengths of field 1

$ nawk '{TMP=length ($1) ; print $TMP}'

netstat - Display Network Status (BSD)

$ **/usr/ucb/netstat** [**–aAn**] [**–f** *addr*] [*system*] [*core*]

$ **/usr/ucb/netstat** [**–himnrs**] [**–f** *addr*] [*system*] [*core*]

$ **/usr/ucb/netstat** [**–n**] [**–I** *inter*] *n* [*system*] [*core*]

Description:

The **netstat** command displays various network statistics.

Options:

–a	display state of all sockets, including servers
–A	display address of protocol control blocks associated with sockets
–h	display state of the IMP host table
–i	display state of the auto-configured interfaces
–f *addr*	list statistics or address control block reports for: **AF_INET** inet **AF_NS** ns **AF_UNIX** unix
–I *inter*	display information for the specified interface
–m	display memory management routine statistics
–n	display network addresses as numbers
–r	display routing tables
–s	display statistics per-protocol
core	specify core file (default **/dev/kmem**)
n	redisplay status every *n* seconds
system	specify object file

newform - Change Text File Format (MISC)

$ newform [–**s**] [*options*] [*files*]

Description:

The **newform** command reformats *files*. Options are processed in the order that they are given.

Options:

–a*n*	append *n* characters to end of line
–b*n*	truncate *n* characters from beginning of line
–c*c*	change the prefix/append character to *c*
–e*n*	truncate *n* characters from end of line
–f	display tab specification format line
–i*ts*	expand tabs to spaces according to the given input tab specifications *ts*. If *ts* is —, input tab specifications are read from standard input. If *ts* is not given, use **–8**. If *ts* is **–0**, and tabs are found, they are treated as **–1**. (see **tabs**)
–l	set line length to 72 characters (default **80**)
–l*n*	set line length to *n* characters
–o*ts*	expand tabs to spaces according to given output tab specifications. If *ts* is —, output tab specifications are read from first line of **stdin**. If *ts* not given, use **–8**. If *ts* is **–0**, and tabs are found, they are treated as **–1**. (see **tabs**)
–p*n*	prepend *n* characters to beginning of the line
–s	move up to 8 characters before first tab to end of the line. If more than 8 characters are removed, the eighth character is replaced with a "*".
files	read standard input if no *files* are specified

Examples:

Display **query.out** with line length set to 60 characters

$ newform –l60 query.out

newgrp - Log In to a New Group (MISC)

$ newgrp [–] [group]

Description:

The **newgrp** command changes the invoker's group ID. If no group is given, invoker is logged into his default group. The invoker is prompted for a password if not a group member, or if group has a password and the invoker does not have a password. **HOME**, **MAIL**, **PS1**, **PS2**, and **PATH** are reset to default values, unless explicitly exported. Other exported variables retain their values.

Options:

–	change to the actual group environment

Examples:

Change group to **sysadm**

$ newgrp sysadm

news - Display News Items (MISC)

$ news [*options*] [*items*]

Description:

The **news** command displays news items from **/var/news**.

Options:

–a	display all news items
–n	display the news item names only
–s	display how many news items exist

Examples:

Display all news items

$ news –a

nice - Run Command at Low Priority (MISC)

$ nice [–*n*] *command* [*arguments*]

 # nice [—*n*] *command* [*arguments*]

Description:

The **nice** command executes *command* with a lower CPU scheduling priority. If no priority is given, priority is lowered by 10. The super-user can raise scheduling priority by preceding priority with two dashes.

Options:

–*n*	lower scheduling priority by *n* (**1–19**)
––*n*	raise scheduling priority by *n* (super-user only)

Examples:

Execute **find** with the scheduling priority lowered by 5

$ nohup nice –5 find . –core –print &

nl - Number Input Lines (FILE)

$ nl [*options*] [*file*]

Description:

The **nl** command displays *file* with numbered lines. Input is read as pages, with each page having a header, body, and footer section. Different line numbering options can be given for each section.

Options:

–b*type*	number *type* lines; *type* can be:
	a — number all lines
	n — do not number lines
	p*exp* — number lines with *exp* only
	t — number lines with printable text onlY
–d*xx*	set start of page section delimiter characters to *xx* (default **\\:**). If only one delimiter character is specified, use "**:**" as the second character.
–f*type*	number *type* lines of the footer (default **n**)
–h*type*	number *type* lines of page header (default **n**)
–i*n*	set line-numbering increment to *n* (default **1**)
–l*n*	treat *n* blank lines as one line (default **1**)
–n*format*	specify line numbering format (default **rn**)
	ln — left justify; strip leading zeroes
	rn — right justify; strip leading zeroes (default)
	rz — right justify (default)
–p	do not restart numbering at page delimiters
–s*c*	separate the line number and text line with character *c* (default **tab**)
–v*n*	number first page *n* (default **1**)
–w*n*	set line number width to *n* characters (default **6**)
file	read standard input if no *file* is specified
format	specifies the line-numbering format for **–n**:

Examples:

Display **file** with all lines numbered

$ nl –ba –p file

Display **rep** with page numbers only; set 1st page to 12

$ nl –bn –v12 rep

nm - Display the Symbol Table of an Object File (PROG)

$ nm [*options*] *files*

Description:

The **nm** command displays the symbol table of the given object files. The name, value, class, type, size, line number, and section for each symbol is displayed.

Options:

–h	do not display the output header
–l	append * to key letter for WEAK symbols
–n	sort external symbols by name
–o	display symbol value and size in octal (default dec)
–p	produce parsable, terse output
–r	prepend object file name to each output line
–u	display undefined symbols only
–v	sort external symbols by value
–V	display version information
–x	display symbol value and size in hex (default dec)

Examples:

Display symbols from **a.out** sorted by external symbol

$ nm –n a.out

nohup - Run Command Ignoring Hangups/Quits (**MISC**)

$ nohup *command* [*arguments*]

Description:

The **nohup** command executes *command* with hangups and quits ignored. If the output is not redirected, the standard output and error are sent to **nohup.out**, or to **$HOME/nohup.out** if the current directory is not writable.

Examples:

\# Execute **find** with hangups and quits ignored

$ nohup find / –type d –print > /tmp/d.out &

\# Execute **backup.sh** with hangups/quits ignored

$ nohup backup.sh &

notify – Notify User of New Mail (**MISC**)

$ notify [*options*]

Description:

The **notify** command informs the invoker that new mail has arrived. It can also be used to save or forward mail to another mailbox. If no options are given, the new mail notification status is displayed.

Options:

–m *file*	save mail messages to *file* (default **$HOME/.mailfile**). If mail cannot be delivered, **notify** checks the **/etc/mail/notify.fsys** file for a directory name that matches the given or default mailfile directory and system to forward it to. If there is no match, mail message is returned.(only with **–y**)
–n	disable mail notification
–y	enable mail notification

Examples:

\# Enable mail notification and save mail to **~/.savemail**

$ notify –y –m ~/.savemail

od - Octal Dump (**MISC**)

$ od [*options*] [*file*] [[**+**]*offset*[**.**][**b**]]

Description:

The **od** command displays *file* according to given format.

Options:

–b	display bytes in octal
–c	display bytes in ASCII. Non-graphic characters appear as escaped characters, others as octal: backspace **\b** null **\0** form-feed **\f** return **\r** new-line **\n** tab **\t**
–d	display bytes in unsigned decimal
–D	display long words in unsigned decimal
–f	display long words in floating point
–F	display double long words in extended precision
–o	display bytes in octal (default)
–O	display long words in unsigned octal

–s	display 16-bit words in signed decimal
–S	display long words in signed decimal
–x	display bytes in hex
–X	display long words in hex

[[+]*offset*[**.**][**b**]]

specify octal *offset* to start the dump:

b	display in 512-byte blocks
.	display in decimal
+	use if no *file* is specified

Examples:

Dump **file** in ASCII format; offset 10 blocks

$ od –c file +10.b

Dump the current directory contents in ASCII format

$ od –c .

openwin - Start Open Windows (SOLARIS)

$ openwin [*options*] [*file*] [[+]*offset*[**.**][**b**]]

Description:

The **openwin** command initializes OpenWindows, the default Solaris windowing environment.

Options:

Xsun and Xserver options also accepted.

–auth *protocol*
use the specified authentication protocol

–includedemo
include demo path in user's search path

–noauth disable user-specific security

–server *server*
start *server* (default is **$OPENWINHOME/bin/Xsun**)

–wm *window-manager*
use the specified window manager (default olwm)

Variables:

DISPLAY specifies server (name or IP address) to use (default ":0")

LD_LIBRARY_PATH
if defined, must be set to **/usr/openwin/lib** (not required)

OPENWINHOME
if defined, must be set to **/usr/openwin** (not required)

OW_WINDOW_MANAGER
specifies an alternate window manager command

XINITRC specifies an initializsation script run after server is up and running. If **$HOME/.xinitrc** does not exist and **XINITRC** not set, **$OPENWINHOME/lib/Xinitrc** is used.

Files:

$HOME/.xinitrc
executed by xinit after server is up and running

$HOME/.Xdefaults
specifies X11 application resource definitions (default **$OPENWINHOME/lib/Xdefaults**)

pack - Compress Files (FILE)

$ pack [–] [**–f**] *files*

Description:

The **pack** command compresses *files*. The compressed file is renamed *file*.**z**. Compressed files can be restored by using **pcat** or **unpack**.

Options:

–	display compression statistics
–f	force packing of *files*

Examples:

\# Pack all C source files in the current directory

$ pack *.c

\# Pack **file.out**; display compression statistics

$ pack – file.out

page - Display Files (BSD)

$ **/usr/ucb/page** [*options*] [–*n*] [+*n*] [+/*pattern*/] [*files*]

Description:

The **page** command displays *files* one screenful at a time.

Options:

–c	redraw each page instead of scrolling
–d	prompt after each page or illegal input (default bell)
–f	count by newlines instead of by screen lines
–l	do not treat **^L** (formfeed) as special character
–s	truncate multiple blank lines into one line
–u	suppress terminal underlining or stand-out mode
–*n*	set window size to *n* lines (default from **stty**)
+*n*	start displaying at line *n*
+/*pat*/	start two lines before line containing pattern *pat*

Commands:

If not specified, the default for *n* is **1**.

[*n*]**b**,[*n*]**B**	go back *n* screenfuls
[*n*]**d**, [n]<Space>	display *n* more lines (default **11**)
^D	display 11 more lines
n^**D**	set scroll size to *n* lines
[*n*]**f**	skip *n* screenfuls
h	display information about **page** commands
q, **Q**	exit from **page**
[*n*]s	skip *n* lines
z	set window size to *n*
v	invoke **vi** at the current line
z	display another screenful
*n***z**	set window size to *n* lines
<space>	display another screenful
=	display current line number
n/*expr*	search for *nth* occurrence of *expr*

*n***n**	search for *nth* occurrence of last *expr*
:f	display current file name and line number
*n***:n**	go to *nth* next file given in the command line
n:p	go to *nth* previous command-line file
.	repeat previous command
!*cmd*	escape to the shell and execute *cmd*

pagesize - Display Size of Memory Page in Bytes (BSD)

$ /usr/ucb/pagesize

Description:

The **pagesize** displays the memory page size in bytes.

passwd - Change Login Password and Attributes (SYSTEM)

$ passwd [–s]

 # passwd [*options*] *user*

Description:

The **passwd** command changes or installs a password or its attributes for the invoker. The super-user can change or install a password or its attributes for any user. Passwords must have at least six characters, and contain at least two alphabetic characters and one numeric or special character. The password cannot be the same as login name, or a circular shift of name. When changing a password, the new password must have at least three different characters than the old password. Only the super-user can enter a null password.

Options:

Except for **–s**, these options are only available to the super-user.

–a	show attributes for all entries (only with **–s**)
–d	delete password for user
–f	force user to change password at next login
–l	lock password entry for user
–n *n*	set minimum number of days between password changes to *n* days. If minimum is greater than maxiumum, then the user cannot change his password.
–s [*name*]	display password attributes for invokers login *name*
–w *n*	warn user *n* days before expiring password
–x *n*	set maximum number of days that password is valid. If maximum is set to **–1**, aging is disabled. If set to **0**, the user much change the password at next login.

Examples:

\# Lock password entry for **psql**

 # passwd –l psql

\# Display password attributes for the invoker

$ passwd –s sa

\# Set the password for **guest**; make it valid for 30 days

$ passwd –x30 guest

paste - Merge Lines Between Files (FILE)

$ paste *file1 file2* **. . .**

$ paste –d*list file1 file2* **. . .**

$ paste –s [**–d***list*] *file1 file2* **. . .**

Description:

The **paste** command merges corresponding lines from *files*. Each file is treated as a columnof a table and displayed horizontally.

Options:

–d*list*	replace tabs with characters from *list*. If this option is not given, newline characters for each file (except for the last file, or if **–s** is given, the last line) are replaced with tabs. The *list* can contain these special characters: **\n** newline **\t** tab **\0** empty string **** backslash
–s	merge subsequent lines instead of one from each file. Use tabs for concatenation, unless **–d***list* is specified.
files	read standard input if *file1*, *file2*, or *files* is –

Examples:

List the contents of the current directory in three columns

$ ls | paste –d" " – – –

List the words in **file** vertically in two columns

$ sed –e 's/ /\\n/' file | paste – –

pcat - Display Compressed Files (FILE)

$ pcat *file*

$ pcat *file***.z**

Description:

The **pcat** command displays the specified compressed file. If *file* is given, **pcat** will search for *file***.z**.

Examples:

Display **hello.c** in uncompressed format

$ pcat hello.c.Z

pg - Display Files (FILE)

$ pg [–*n*] [**–p** *string*] [**–cefns**] [+*n*] [**+/***pattern***/**] [*files*]

Description:

The **pg** command displays the specified files one screenful at a time. Display commands can be given at the prompt.

Options:

–c	clear the screen before displaying each page
–e	do not pause between files
–f	do not split lines longer than the screen width

–n read commands without waiting for the newline

–p *string* use *string* as prompt. If *string* contains **%d**, prompt is replaced with the current page number. (default **:**)

–r disallow shell escapes

–s display messages and prompts in inverse video

–n set screen size to *n* lines (default **23**)

+*n* start at line *n*

+/*pattern*/ start at first line containing *pattern*

Commands:

Commands are entered at prompt. If not given, *n* defaults to **1**.

[*n*] **d**, [*n*]**^D**
scroll from line *n*

[+*n*] **d**, [+*n*]**^D**
scroll forward *n* half screens

[–*n*] **d**, [–*n*]**^D**
scroll backward *n* half screens

h display abbreviated summary of commands

[*n*] **l** scroll from line *n*

[+*n*] **l** scroll forward *n* lines

[–*n*] **l** scroll backward *n* lines

^L redisplay current page

[*n*] **n** display *nth* next command line file

[*n*] **p** display *nth* previous command line file

q, **Q** quit

s *file* save to *file*

[*n*] **w** set the window size to *n*.

[*n*] <Return>, [*n*] <Space>
display the first *n* pages

[+*n*]<Return>, [+*n*]<Space>
display next *n* pages

[–*n*]<Return>, [–*n*]<Space>
display previous *n* pages

[*n*] /*pattern*/
search forward for *nth* occurrence of *pattern*

[*n*] ^*pattern*^, [*n*] ?*pattern*?
search backward for *nth* occurrence of *pattern*

. redisplay current page

$ display last page

!*cmd* escape to shell and execute *cmd*

Variables:

SHELL contains name of current shell (used for shell escape)

TERM contains name of terminal type (default **dumb**)

Examples:

Display the given files one page at a time; clear between pages

$ pg –c /etc/passwd /etc/group

Display **file**; set prompt to "**Press <Space> to continue**"

$ pg –p "Press <Space> to continue" file portrait)

pr - Display Files (FILE)

$ pr [*options*] [*files*]

Description:

The **pr** command displays *files* according to the given format options. If no *options* are specified, the default file format is 66 line page length with a 5 line header and a 5 line trailer. The default header contains the page number, the file name, and the last modification date and time.

Options:

–a	display multi-column output across the page. Lines that cannot fit in a column are truncated. (not with **–m**)
–d	double-space the output
–e*kn*	expand input tabs to every *nth* position using *k* as tab character (default *n* is **8**, and *k* is **tab**)
–f	use single form-feed character for new pages
–F	fold input lines to fit in current column width
–h*string*	use *string* instead of file name in the header
–i*kn*	convert whitespace to tabs every*nth* position using k as tab character (default *n* is **8**, and *k* is **tab**)
–l*n*	set the page length to *n* lines. If *n* is less than **11**, the headers and trailers are not displayed. (default **66**)
–m	display all files, one per column. The maximum number of files is eight. (not with **–a** or **–***n*)
–n*cn*	use *n*-digit line numbering and append character *c* to the line number (default *n* is **5**, and *c* is **tab**)
–o*n*	offset each line by *n* characters (default **0**)
–p	pause between pages
–r	do not display warning or error messages
–s*c*	set the column separator to *c* (default **tab**)
–t	do not display headers or trailers (overrides **–h**)
–w*n*	set the line width to *n* characters (default **72**)
–*n*	produce *n* column output (default **1**, not with **–m**)
+*n*	begin display at page *n* (default **1**)
files	read standard input if *files* is **–**, or no *files* are specified

Examples:

Display **file** with the banner **1992** and set the page length to 45

$ pr –l45 –w60 –h"1992" file

Display **file1** with line numbers; do not use headers or trailers

$ pr –n –t file1

Display **file** in two-column format

$ pr –2 file

printenv - Display Environment Variable Values (BSD)

$ **/usr/ucb/printenv** [*variable*]

Description:

The **printenv** command displays the value for *variable*. If no *variable* specified, display the values for all environment variables.

printf, prof, prs

printf – Format Output (MISC)

$ printf *format* [*args*]

Description:

The **printf** command displays *args* according to *format*, which can consist of character strings, %s string conversion specifications, %% to display %, or C language escape sequences.

Examples:

Display the **HOME** variable and its value

$ printf 'HOME variable is set to %s\n' $HOME

prof - Display Profile Data (PROG)

$ prof [*options*] [*objfile*]

Description:

The **prof** command displays profile data for the specified object file. The number of function calls, average milliseconds per call, and the percentage of time spent executing between the address of each symbol is displayed.

Options:

–a	sort by increasing symbol addresses
–c	sort by decreasing number of calls
–g	include all non-global symbols
–h	do not display report heading
–l	do not include static functions (default)
–m*file*	use *file* instead of **mon.out**
–n	sort lexically by symbol name
–o	display symbol name and address in octal format
–s	display a summary of statistics
–t	sort by decreasing percentage of execution time (default)
–V	display version information
–x	display symbol name and address in hex format
–z	include all symbols in the profile range
objfile	specify name of the object file (default **a.out**)

Examples:

Display summary profile data for **satool**

$ prof –s satool

prs - Display an SCCS File (SCCS)

$ prs [*options*] *files*

Description:

The **prs** command displays parts or all of the specified SCCS files according to *options*. If *files* is a directory, then all files in that directory that begin with **s.** are processed.

Options:

–a	display information for removed and existing deltas
–c[*date*]	specify date for **–e** and **–l**
–d[*fmt*]	specify output format (can contain SCCS data keywords with optional text)

–e	display info about older newer than from **–r** or **–c**
–l	display info about deltas newer than from **–r** or **–c**
–r	display information for the most recently created delta
–r[*delta*]	display information for the specified delta
date	format is *yy[mm[dd[hh[mm[ss]]*
files	file names beginning with **s.**, **–**, or directory names. If *files* is a directory, then all files in the directory beginning with **s.** are processed. If *files* is –, read file names from **stdin**.

Data Keywords:

:A:	type of WHAT string **:Z::Y: :M: :I::Z:**	
:B:	branch	*number*
:BD:	body	*text*
:C:	comments	*text*
:D:	creation date	**:Dy:/:Dm:/:Dd:**
:Dd:	creation day	*number*
:DI:	all delta sequence numbers	**:Dn:/:Dx:/:Dg:**
:DL:	line statistics	**:Li:/:Ld:/:Lu:**
:DM:	creation month	*number*
:Dn:	included deltas	**:DS: :DS: . . .**
:Ds:	default delta ID	**:I:**
:DS:	delta sequence number	*number*
:Dt:	delta information	**:DT::I::D::T::P::DS::DP:**
:DT:	type	**D** or **R**
:Dy:	creation year	*number*
:F:	file name	*text*
:FD:	file descriptive text	*text*
:FL:	flag list	*text*
:GB:	retrieved body	*text*
:I:	SCCS ID string.	**:R:.:L:.:B:.:S:**
:KF:	keyword error flag	**yes** or **no**
:L:	level	*number*
:Ld:	lines deleted	*number*
:Li:	lines inserted	*number*
:LK:	locked releases	**:R:...**
:Lu:	lines unchanged	*number*
:M:	module name	*text*
:MF:	MR validation flag	**yes** or **no**
:MP:	MR validation program	*text*
:MR:	MR numbers	*text*
:P:	programmer name	*login name*
:PN:	file path name	*text*
:R:	release	*number*
:S:	sequence	*number*
:T:	creation time	**:Th:::Tm:::Ts:**
:Th:	creation hour	*number*
:Tm:	creation minute	*number*
:UN:	user names *text*	
W:	type of WHAT string **:Z::M::\t:I:**	
:Z:	WHAT delimiter	**@(#)**

Examples:

\# Display the comment field for all deltas for **s.hello.c**

```
$ prs –d":C:" s.hello.c
```

\# Display the programmer name for each delta in **s.file**

```
$ prs –d"Made by :P:" s.file
```

ps - Report Process Status (SYSTEM, BSD)

$ ps [*options*]

$ /usr/ucb/ps [*options*] [*nlist*] [*core*] [*swap*] [**t***list*] [*process-number*]

Description:

The **ps** command displays information about active processes according to *options*. If no *options* given, information is displayed about processes associated with current terminal only.

Options:

–a	display information about all processes except process group leaders, and those not associated with a terminal
–c	include schedule priority information
–d	display information about all running processes, except process group leaders
–e	display information about all running processes
–f	generate a full listing
–g *list*	display information about processes associated with process group leaders in *list*
–j	display session ID and process group ID
–l	generate a long listing
–p *list*	display information about processes associated with process ID's in *list*
–s *list*	display information about processes with session leaders from *list*
–t *list*	display information about processes associated with terminals in *list*. Terminals can be specified with the device file name or just the numeric portion if the device file name begins with **tty**.
–u *list*	display information about processes associated with user ID's or user names in *list*
list	items can be separated with commas, or enclosed in double quotes and separated with commas or spaces

BSD Options:

a	display information about processes with terminals
c	display the command name as stored internally
e	display the environment and command arguments
g	display information about all processes
k	use **/vmcore** instead of **/dev/kmem** and **/dev/mem**
l	display information using long format
n	display **WCHAN** and **USER** fields numerically
s	add kernel stack size to output
t*list*	list processes associated with terminals in *list* (this must be the last option specified)
u	display information with user-oriented format
U	update a private database
v	display virtual memory statistics information
w	use 132-column wide output format
ww	use arbitrarily wide output format
x	include processes with no terminal
nlist	use system namelist file *nlist* (default **/vmunix**)
swap	use the specified swap file (default **/dev/drum**)

Column Headings:

ADDR	memory address of the process
C	processor utilization for scheduling
CLS	scheduling class
COMMAND	command name
F	flags associated with the process
NI	nice value
PID	process ID
PPID	parent process ID
PRI	process priority
S	process state
STIME	process start time
SZ	process size
TIME	cumulative execution time for the process
TTY	controlling terminal for the process
UID	user ID of the process owner
WCHAN	event address for which process is waiting

Examples:

Display info for processes associated with user ID **112**, **125**

$ ps –u 112,125

Display all information for associated with **/dev/tty07**

$ ps –lt 07

pwd - Display Current Working Directory (**MISC**)

$ pwd

Description:

The **pwd** command displays the name of the current directory.

quota - Display Disk Usage and Limits for Users (**BSD**)

$ /usr/ucb/quota [*options*] [*user*]

Description:

The **quota** command shows invokers disk usage and limits.

Options:

–q	display information about file systems where usage exceeds quota
–v	display quotas for file systems where no storage is allocated for invoker

rcp - Copy Remote Files (**FILE, BSD**)

$ rcp [**–p**] *file1* [*file2* | *directory*]

$ /usr/ucb/rcp [**–pr**] *files* [*file2* | *directory*]

Description:

The **rcp** command copies files between systems. Remote file or directory arguments are given with the format: *rhost:pathname*, *user@host:file*, or *user@host.domain:file*, where *file* is interpreted relative to the invokers or users home directory on the remote host if a full pathname is not given.

Options:

–p	duplicate modification times and modes of the source files
–r	recursively copy *directory* and its subdirectories
file	specify file with format *rhost:pathname*. If *pathname* not absolute, it is interpreted relative to invoker's login directory on *rhost*.

Examples:

\# Copy **file** to the **/usr/tmp** directory on **mhost**

$ rcp file mhost:/usr/tmp

\# Copy **/usr/src** and all of its contents to **/home/src** on **demosys**

$ rcp –r /usr/src demosys:/home/src

rdist - Remote File Distribution Program (**BSD**)

$ /usr/ucb/rdist [**–bhinqRvwy**] [**–f** *dfile*] [**–d** *var=v*] [**–m** *host*][*files*]

$ /usr/ucb/rdist [**–bhinqRvwy**] [**–c** *files*] [*login@*]*host* [**:***dest*]

Description:

The **rdist** command updates *files* over multiple hosts. If no *files* specified, all files updated from *dfile*, otherwise files are interpreted as files to update or command labels to execute.

Options:

–b	perform a binary comparison and update if they are different (default compare dates and sizes)
–c *files* [*login@*]*host*[**:***dest*]	update *files* on *host* as *login* and install as *dest*. If no *login* given, use current login. If no *dest* file given, use source file name.
–d*var=v*	define *var* to *v*; command-line variable assignments override variable definitions in dfile
–f *dfile*	read commands from *dfile*. If *dfile* is **–**, then read commands from **stdin**. (default **distfile**, **Distfile**)
–h	copy the file that link points to rather than the link
–i	ignore unresolved links
–m *host*	update *host* only (multiple **–m**'s allowed)
–n	display commands without executing them
–q	do not display file names when modifying
–R	remove files from directories on remote host if they do not exist in the master directory
–v	verify that files are up to date on all hosts. Display out of date file names, but do not update.
–w	append the entire file name to destination directory name instead of just the last component
–y	do not update files younger than the master copy

regcmp - Compile Regular Expressions (**PROG**)

$ regcmp [**–**] *files*

Description:

The **regcmp** command compiles the regular expressions from *files* and places the output in *file*.**i**.

Options:

–	place the output in *file*.**c** (default *file*.**i**)

relogin - Rename Login Entry for Current Layer (**MISC**)

$ /usr/lib/layersys/relogin [–s] *line*

Description:

The **relogin** command modifies the terminal *line* of the invoker's **utmp** entry to the layer attached to standard input.

Options:

–s	do not display error messages
line	specify which tty field to change

reset - Reset Terminal to Normal Mode (**BSD**)

$ /usr/ucb/reset

rlogin - Login to Remote System (**SYSTEM, BSD**)

$ rlogin [*options*] *system*

$ /usr/ucb/rlogin [*options*] *system*

Description:

The **rlogin** command logs the invoker onto the remote *system*. The invoker is prompted for a password, unless remote account is not the same as current account, and system not in remote **/etc/hosts.equiv** file. A user can login to remote system as different user without being prompted for a password if the remote **~/.rhosts** file contains the hsotname and user name of the local user.

Options:

–e*c*	set escape character to *c* (default ~)
–l *user*	login as *user* instead of the current user
–L	run **rlogin** session in litout mode
–8	pass 8-bit data across the network

Example:

\# Login to **mhost** as **sadmin**

$ rlogin –l sadmin mhost

rm - Remove Files or Directories (**FILE**)

$ rm [**–f**] [**–i**] *files*

$ rm –r [**–f**] [**–i**] *directories* [*files*]

Description:

The **rm** command removes the given files or directories. Write permission for the directory is required to remove files from it. If a file does not have write permission, the invoker is prompted for a confirmation. If the reply begins with **y**, the file is deleted.

Options:

–f	force removal of the files if write-protected; do not prompt for confirmation. If the directory that contains the files is not writable, the files are not removed.
–i	interactively remove files
–r	recursively delete the contents of *directories*

Example:

\# Remove the **/usr/src/junk** directory and all of its contents

$ rm –rf /usr/src/junk

rmdel, rmdir, rsh

rmdel - Remove a Delta from an SCCS File (**SCCS**)

$ rmdel –r*SID files*

Description:

The **rmdel** command removes the delta given by SID from the given SCCS files. If *files* is a directory, then all files in that directory that begin with **s.** are processed.

Options:

–r*SID*	remove *SID*. The delta must be the most recent, and cannot be one that is being edited to make a delta.
files	file names beginning with **s.**, **–**, or directory names. If *files* is a directory, then all files in the directory beginning with **s.** are processed. If *files* is –, read file names from **stdin**.

Examples:

Determine, then remove the most recent delta for **s.file**

```
$SID=`prs –d:I: s.file`; rmdel –r$SID s.file
```

rmdir - Remove Directories (**FILE**)

$ rmdir [**–p**] [**–s**] *directories*

Description:

The **rmdir** command removes directories. Directories must be empty to be removed.

Options:

–p	remove parent directories also
–s	do not display error messages

Examples:

Remove **/usr/tmp/src/junk** and empty parent directories also

```
$ rmdir –p /usr/tmp/src/junk
```

rsh - Remote Shell (**MISC, BSD**)

$ rsh *system* [*options*] [*command*]

$ /usr/ucb/rsh *system* [*options*] [*command*]

$ *hostname* [*options*] [*command*]

Description:

The **rsh** command executes *command* on remote *system*. If *command* is not given, then log into system via **rlogin**.

Options:

–l *user*	login as *user* instead of the current user
–n	redirect input of **rsh** from **/dev/null**
command	login to remote if *command* not specified

Examples:

Display the remote **/etc/passwd** file from **mhost**

```
$ rsh mhost cat /etc/passwd
```

ruptime - Report Status of Local Machines (**SYSTEM, BSD**)

$ **ruptime** [*options*]

$ **/usr/ucb/ruptime** [*options*]

Description:

The **ruptime** command displays the status for systems on the local network. If no *options* given, display the status sorted by host name.

Options:

–a	include users with more than one hour of idle time
–l	display status sorted by load average
–r	reverse the sort order
–t	display status sorted by uptime
–u	display status sorted by number of users

Examples:

Display local network status sorted by number of users

$ **ruptime –u**

rwho - Display Who Is Logged on the Local Network (**SYSTEM, BSD**)

$ **rwho** [**–a**]

$ **/usr/ucb/rwho** [**–a**]

Description:

The **rwho** command shows who is logged on systems on the local network.

Options:

–a	include users who have been inactive for one hour or more

sact - Display Current SCCS File Editing Activity (**SCCS**)

$ **sact** *files*

Description:

The **sact** command reports of any impending deltas to the specified SCCS files. The files can be file names beginning with **s.**, directory names, or –. If *files* is a directory, then all files in the directory whose names begin with **s.** are processed. Read file or directory names from standard input if *files* is –.

Examples:

Check if there is any activity on SCCS files in **/usr/lib/source**

$ **sact /usr/lib/source**

sccs - Execute SCCS Commands (**BSD**)

$ **/usr/ucb/sccs** [*options*] *command* [*flags*] [*files*]

Description:

The **sccs** command executes the special or actual SCCS commands.

Options:

–d*dir*	use *dir* for the root directory for SCCS files (default current directory)
–r	execute **sccs** as the real user

–p*dir*	get SCCS files from *dir*; insert *dir* before the final component of the pathname (default **SCCS**)
command	**sccs** command or actual SCCS command:

check	return nonzero exit code if file is being edited
clean	remove files that aren't being edited via SCCS
create	create SCCS files (same as **admin –i, get**)
deledit	same as **delta** followed by **get –e**
delget	same as **delta** followed by **get**
diffs	compare current and SCCS version of *file*
edit	edit a file (same as **get –e**)
enter	same as **admin –i**
fix	same as **rmdel**
info	show files being edited
print	same as **prs –e**, **get –p –m**
tell	same as info, but show one filename per line
unedit	same as **unget**

files	**SCCS/s.** is usually prepended to files
flags	flags for SCCS commands come after command

sccsdiff - Compare Two Versions of an SCCS File (SCCS)

$ sccsdiff –r*delta* **–r***delta* [*options*] *files*

Description:

The **sccsdiff** command displays the differences (in **diff** format) between the two versions of the given SCCS files.

Options:

–p	send the output through **pr**
–r*delta*	specify the deltas to be compared
–s*n*	set file segment size to *n*

Examples:

Compare the differences between versions **1.1** and **1.2** of **s.file**

$ sccsdiff –r1.1 –r1.2 s.file | pg

script - Create Typescript of Terminal Session (MISC, BSD)

$ script [**–a**] [*file*]

$ /usr/ucb/script [**–a**] [*file*]

Description:

The **script** command copies everything displayed on the terminal to *file*. If no *file* specified, output is copied to **typescript**. Copying is terminated on **^D** or **exit**.

Options:

–a	append output to *file*
file	send output to *file* (default **typescript**)

Examples:

Run **ftp** session and save output in **ftp.script**

$ script ftp uunet.uu.net ftp.script

sdb - Symbolic Debugger (PROG)

$ sdb *[options] [objfile[corefile [dir-list]]]*

Description:

The **sdb** command debugs C and assembler language programs. Object files should be compiled with the **–g** option.

Options:

–e	ignore symbolic information
–s *n*	do not stop process if signal *n* received
–V	display version information
–w	allow overwriting of *objfile*
–W	disable checking and suppress warnings
corefile	specify the core image file. If *corefile* is **–**, ignore the core image file. (default **core**)
dir-list	list of colon-separated search directories
objfile	specifies the executable file (default **a.out**)

sdiff - Show File Differences Side-by-Side (FILE)

$ sdiff *[options] file1 file2*

Description:

The **sdiff** command displays differences between two files. The two files are displayed side by side with differences marked between them. A blank indicates identical lines, **|** indicates different lines, **<** indicates line is only in *file1*, and **>** indicates line is only in *file2*.

Options:

–l display the left side of identical lines only

–o *file* interactively merge *file1* and *file2* in *file*. The invoker is prompted with **%** for one of the following commands:

e	invoke editor with empty file
e b	invoke editor with right & left column
e l	invoke editor with the left column
e r	invoke editor with the right column
l	append left column to the output file
q	exit from **sdiff**
r	append right column to output file
s	do not display identical lines
v	display identical lines

–s do not display identical lines

–w *n* set the output line width to *n* (default **130**)

Examples:

Interactively merge **a.c b.c** and put output in **rep.c**

```
$ sdiff –o rep.c a.c b.c
```

sed - Stream Editor (MISC)

$ sed [–n] [–e '*script*' [–f *file*] [*files*]

Description:

The **sed** command copies *files* to standard output and edits them according to the given editing commands.

Options:

–e *script*	execute commands in *script*
–f *file*	get commands from *file*
–n	suppress default output
files	read standard input if no *files* are specified

Command Format:

[*address* [,*address*]] *commands* [*arguments*]

execute *commands* for each input line that matches *address* or range of addresses. If *commands* is preceded by **!**, input lines that do not match the address are used.

address	number of lines, **$** for the last line, or regular expression

Commands:

The maximum number of addresses is listed in parentheses.

(1)a *text*	append following text to output
(2)b *label*	branch to **:***label*. If *label* is empty, go to end of script.
(2)c *text*	change lines
(2)d	delete lines
(2)D	delete first line of input only
(2)g	replace lines with the buffer contents
(2)G	append buffer contents to input lines
(2)h	replace buffer contents with input lines
(2)H	append input lines to buffer contents
(1)i *text*	insert following text
(2)l	display input lines
(2)n	display input line; read next input line
(2)N	append next input line to current line
(2)p	display input lines
(2)P	display first line of input line only
(1)q	quit
(2)r*file*	display contents of file

(2)s/*RE***/***s***/***flags*

substitute *s* for regular expression RE that match input lines according to *flag* and can consist of zero or more of:

n	substitute for *nth* occurrence of RE **(1–512)**
g	substitute for all occurrences or RE
p	display input line if substitution was made
w *file*	append line with substitution to *file*

(2)t *label*	branch to the **:***label* command if substitution was made. If *label* is empty, go to end of script.
(2)w*file*	append input line to *file*

(2)x	exchange input line with buffer contents
(2)y/*s1***/***s2*	replace characters in *s1* with characters in *s2*
(2)!*cmd*	execute command for input lines not selected
(1) =	display current line number
(2) {	treat commands up to closing } as a group
(0)#	interpret rest of input line as comments
(0)#n	interpret rest of the input line as comments and ignore

Examples:

\# Substitute all occurrences of **The** with **A** in **file**

$ sed 's/The/A/g' file

\# Display your user name only

$ id | sed 's/).*//' | sed 's/.*(//'

\# Display the first 75 lines of **file1**

$ sed 75q file1

\# Display **file** with lines that contain **string** deleted

$ sed '/string/d' file

sh/jsh/rsh- Bourne Shell Command Interpreter (MISC)

$ sh [*options*] [*arguments*]

Description:

The **sh** command is a Bourne shell command programming language interpreter. It executes commands read from a terminal or file. The **rsh** command is a restricted version of **sh** that provides a more limited execution environment. The **jsh** command provides the same functionality as **sh** and enables job control.

Options:

Options can be preceded with **+** instead of – to disable flags.

–a	automatically export variables that are defined
–c *cmds*	read and execute commands
–e	exit if a command fails
–f	disable file name expansion
–h	remember functions on definition instead of on execution
–i	execute in interactive mode
–k	put variable assignment arguments in environment
–n	read commands without executing them
–p	do not set effective ids to real ids
–r	run a restricted shell
–s	read commands from standard input
–t	exit after reading and executing one command
–u	return error on substitution of unset variables
–v	display input lines as they are read
–x	display commands and arguments as executed
– –	do not change any of the flags (used to set **$1** to –)

Command Execution Format:

cmd1 **;** *cmd2*	execute *cmd1* followed by *cmd2*
cmd **&**	execute *cmd* asynchronously in the background

cmd1 | *cmd2*
  pass **stdout** of *cmd1* to **stdin** of *cmd2*

cmd1 && *cmd2*
  execute *cmd2* if *cmd1* returns zero exit status

cmd1 || *cmd2*
  execute *cmd2* if *cmd1* returns non-zero exit status

cmd \ — continue *cmd* onto the next line

{ *cmd*; } — execute *cmd* in the current shell

(*cmd*) — execute *cmd* in a subshell

name() { *commands* ; }
  define a function *name* associated with *commands*

Input/Output & Process Execution:

<file — redirect standard input from *file*

>file — redirect standard output to *file*. Create *file* if non-existent, else overwrite.

>>file — append standard output to *file*; create if non-existent.

<&- — close standard input

>&- — close standard output

<&*n* — redirect standard input from file descriptor *n*

>&*n* — redirect standard output to file descriptor *n*

n<file — redirect file descriptor *n* from *file*

n>file — redirect file descriptor *n* to *file*

n>>file — redirect file descriptor *n* to *file*. Create *file* if non-existent, else overwrite.

n<&*m* — redirect file descriptor *n* from file descriptor *m*

n>&*m* — redirect file descriptor *n* to file descriptor *m*

n<<*x* — redirect to file descriptor *n* until *x* is read

n<<–*x* — same as *n*<<*x*, except ignore leading tabs

n<&– — close file descriptor *n* for standard input

n>&– — close file descriptor *n* for standard output

File Name Variables:

? — match any single character

* — match zero or more characters, including null

[abc] — match any characters between the brackets

[x–z] — match any character or characters in the range **x** to **z**

[a–ce–g] — match any characters in the range **a** to **c**, **e** to **g**

[!abc] — match any characters not between the brackets

[!x–z] — match any characters not in the range **x** to **z**

. — strings starting with **.** must be explicitly matched

Quote Characters:

'...' — remove the special meaning of enclosed characters except **'**

"..." — remove special meaning of enclosed characters except **$**, **'**, **"**, and ****

c — remove special meaning of character *c*

\`*cmd*\` — replace with standard output of *cmd*

Job Control Commands:

bg [%*n*] — put current or stopped job *n* in the background

fg [%*n*] — move current or background job *n* into foreground

jobs — display status of all jobs

jobs –l display status of all jobs along with their process ids

jobs –p display process ids of all jobs

jobs –x *command*
: replace job *n* in *command* with the corresponding process group id, then execute *command*

kill [–*signal*] %*n*
: send specified signal to job *n* (default **9**)

stop %*n* stop job *n*

stty [–]**tostop**
: allow/prevent background jobs from generating output

suspend suspend execution of the current shell

wait wait for all background jobs to complete

wait %*n* wait for background job *n* to complete

Ctl-z stop current job

Job Name Format

%%, *%+*	current job
%n	job *n*
%–	previous job
%string	job whose name begins with *string*
%?string	job that matches part or all of *string*

Variable Assignment Format:

variable=, *variable=""*
: declare *variable* and set it to null

variable=value
: assign *value* to *variable*

Variable Evaluation:

If colon is omitted from these, variable is only checked if it is set.

$*var*	value of variable *var*
${*var*}	value of delimited variable *var*
${*var:–s*}	value of *var* if set and not null, else value of *s*
${*var:=s*}	value of *var* if set and not null, else set *var* to *s*
${*var:?*}	value of *var* if set and not null, else display ***var*: parameter null or not set**
${*var:?s*}	value of *var* if set and not null, otherwise display value of *s* and exit
${*var:+s*}	value of *s* if *var* set and not null, else null value

Special Variables:

CDPATH contains search path for **cd** when not given full pathname

HOME default argument for **cd** ; contains pathname of home directory

IFS contains internal field separators (default newline, space, tab)

LANG contains name of current locale

MAIL contains name of file to check for mail if **MAILPATH** is not set

MAILCHECK
: specifies how often in seconds to check for mail in **$MAIL** or **$MAILPATH**. If set to zero, mail is checked before each prompt. (default **600** seconds)

MAILPATH
: contains a list of colon-separated file names that are checked for mail. Files can be followed by **%** and a message to display each time new mail is received. (default message "**you have mail**")

PATH	contains a list of colon-separated pathnames to search for commands. Current directory specified by "**:**" and paths are searched from left to right.
PS1	contains primary prompt string (default **$**)
PS2	contains secondary prompt string (default **>**)
SHACCT	contains name of file to use for writing accounting records to for each shell procedure
SHELL	contains name of current shell
TERM	specifies your terminal type (no default)
?	contains exit status of last non-background executed command
#	contains number of positional parameters
$	contains process ID of the current shell
!	contains process ID of last background invoked command
–	contains shell flags from **set** or invocation
n	contains current shell argument *n* (**1–9**)
0	contains name of the current shell name
*	contains args referenced as **$1**, **$2**, **$3**, . . .
@	contains args referenced as "**$1**", "**$2**", "**$3**", . . .

Control Commands:

case *word* **in**
pattern) *commands*;;
pattern) *commands*;;
. . .
*) *commands*;;
esac

Execute *commands* associated with the *pattern* that matches *word*. If *pattern* is *, its *commands* are executed if no other match is obtained. If two *patterns* are separated with |, then match on either pattern. The format for patterns is the same as for file name generation, except that /, ., and /. do not have to be matched explicitly.

for *variable*
do
commands
done
for *var* **;** **do** *commands* **;** **done**

Execute *commands* once for each positional parameter, setting *var* to successive positional parameters each time. The second listing shows the format when giving the command on one line.

for *variable* **in** *word1 word2* **. . .** *wordn*
do
commands
done
for *var* **in** *word1 word2* **. . .** *wordn* **;** **do** *commands* **;** **done**

Execute *commands* once for each *word*, setting *var* to successive *wordn* each time. Second listing shows format when specifying the command on one line.

if *expression*
then
    commands
fi
if *expression* **; then** *commands* **; fi**

Execute *commands* if *expression* returns a zero exit status (true). Second listing shows format when giving the command on one line.

if *expression*
then
    commands1
else
    commands2
fi
if *expression* **; then** *commands1* **; else** *commands2* **; fi**

Execute *commands1* if *expression* returns a zero exit status (true), otherwise execute *commands2*. The second listing shows the format when specifying the command on one line.

if *exp1*
then
    cmds1
elif *exp2*
then
    cmds2. . .
else
    cmds3
fi
if *exp1***; then** *cmds1***; elif** *exp2***; then** *cmds2. . .* **; else** *cmds3***; fi**

Execute *cmds1* if *exp1* returns a zero exit status, otherwise execute *cmds2* if *exp2* returns a zero exit status, and so on. Execute *cmds3* if *exp2* returns a non-zero zero exit status. The second listing shows the format when specifying the command on one line.

until *expression*
do
    commands
done
until *expression* **; do** *commands* **; done**

Execute *commands* until *expression* returns a zero exit status (true). Second line shows format to use when giving command on one line.

while *expression*
do
    commands
done,
while *expression* **; do** *commands* **; done**

Execute *commands* while *expression* returns a zero exit status. Second listing shows format to use when giving command on 1 line.

Special Commands:

:	null command; returns zero exit status
. *file*	read/execute commands from *file* in current environment
#	begin comments; terminate with a newline
break	exit from current enclosing **for**, **until**, or **while** loop
break *n*	exit from the *nth* enclosing **for**, **until**, or **while** loop
cd *dir*	change directory to *dir*. If *dir* not specified, change directory to **$HOME**.
echo *arguments*	display *arguments*
eval *command*	evaluate *command* and execute the result
exec *command*	replace current process with *command*
exit	exit from current program with exit status of last command. If given at command prompt, terminate shell.
exit *n*	exit from the current program with exit status *n*
export	display list of exported variables
export *variable*	export *variable*
getopts	parse positional parameters and options
hash	display a list of hashed commands
hash *commands*	remember locations of *commands* by putting them in hash table
hash –r	remove all commands from the hash table
hash –r *command*	remove *command* from the hash table
newgrp	change group-id to default group-id
newgrp *gid*	change group id to *gid*
pwd	display pathname of current directory
read *variables*	read a line from standard input; assign each word on line to each variable. Words delimited with **IFS**.
readonly	display list of readonly variables
readonly *variable*	set *variable* to be readonly
return	exit from function with a return status of last command
return *n*	exit from a function with return status *n*
set	display list of current variables and their values
set *args*	set positional parameters to *args*
set *–args*	set positional parameters even if they begin with –
set [*options*]	enable/disable options (see **Options**)
shift	shift positional parameters once left
shift *n*	shift positional parameters *n* times left
test *expression*	evaluate *expression* (see **test** command)
times	display total user/system time for current shell and its child processes
trap	display list of current traps

trap *commands signals*
: execute *commands* when *signals* are received

trap "" *signals*
: ignore *signals*

trap *signals*, **trap** *–signals*
: reset traps to their default values

trap *commands* **0**
: execute *commands* on exit from the shell

type *command*
: display information and location for *command*

ulimit [*type*] [*options*] *n*
: set a resource limit to *n*. If *n* is not given, the specified resource limit is displayed.If no *option* is given, the file size limit (**–f**) is displayed. If no *type* is given, both limits are set, or soft limit is displayed; *type* can be:

–H	hard limit
–S	soft limit

and *options* can be:

–a	displays all current resource limits
–c *n*	set core dump size limit to *n* 512-byte blocks
–d *n*	set data area size limit to *n* kilobytes
–f *n*	set child process file write limit to *n*
512-byte	blocks (default)
–m *n*	set physical memory size limit to *n* kilobytes
–s *n*	set stack area size limit to *n* kilobytes
–t *n*	set process time limit to *n* seconds
–v*n*	set virtual memory size to *n* kilobytes

umask display current value of the file creation mask

umask *mask*
: set default file creation mask to octal *mask*

unset *variable*
: remove definition of *variable*

wait [*n*] wait for execution (see **Job Control** section)

Invocation:

These flags are available to the shell on invocation only:

–c *string*	execute the commands from *string*
–i	execute in interactive mode
–r	invoke a restricted shell
–s	read commands from standard input

Restricted Shell:

This is a restricted version of the shell. Changing directories, specifying path or command names using **/**, setting **PATH**, and redirecting output is not allowed.

Files:

$HOME/.profile
: contains local environment settings. At login time, it is read in and executed after the **/etc/profile** file.

/etc/profile contains system-wide environment settings. If existent, it is read in and executed before **$HOME/.profile**.

shl, size, sleep

shl - Shell Layer Manager (MISC)

$ shl

Description:

The **shl** command allows the user to interact with multiple shells (called **layers**) from a single terminal. The **stty** character **swtch** is used to switch control to **shl** from a layer. It has its own prompt **>>>**.

Commands:

create[*layer*]
: create *layer* and make it the current layer. If no layer name is specified, use last digit of virtual device bound to layer as the name.

block *layers*
: block output of *layers*

delete *layers*
: delete the *layers*

help, **?** display syntax for the **shl** commands

layers [**–l**] [*layers*]
: list layers and their process groups. If **–l** is given, generate long listing. If no *layers* are given , list all existing layers.

quit exit **shl**

resume [*layer*]
: make *layer* the current layer

toggle make previous current layer the current layer

unblock *layers*
: unblock output of *layers*

layer make *layer* the current layer

Variables:

SHELL contains pathname of the shell to use (default **/bin/sh**)

size - Display Size of Object File (FILE)

$ size [*options*] *files*

Description:

The **size** command displays the size of the text, data, and bss sections and the total size of the specified object files. If an archive file is given, information for all the members is displayed.

Options:

–f include information for each allocatable section

–F include information for each loadable segment

–n include information for non-allocatable sections or non-loadable segments

–o display numbers in octal (default decimal)

–V display version information

–x display numbers in hexadecimal (default decimal)

sleep - Suspend Execution (MISC)

$ sleep *n*

Description:

The **sleep** command suspends execution for *n* seconds.

sort - Sort-Merge Files (FILE)

$sort [*options*] [*files*]

Description:

The **sort** command sorts lines from *files*. The sorting is based on one or more sort keys from each input line.

Options:

–b	ignore leading tabs and spaces. If **–b** is specified before the first **+***pos1* argument, it is applied to all **+***pos1* arguments, otherwise it can be applied to all *pos* arguments.
–c	check that input is in sorted order
–d	sort in dictionary order; only letters, digits, and white-space are significant in comparisons
–f	sort upper and lower case letters together
–i	ignore non-printable characters
–m	merge already sorted files
–M	sort as months; the first three non-blank characters are converted to upper case and compared (implies **–b**)
–n	sort by numerical value; blanks, minus signs, and decimal points can also be given (implies **–b**)
–o*file*	send output to *file* (default standard output)
–r	reverse the sort order
–t*c*	set field separator to *c*
–u	display only one occurrence of duplicate lines
–y*k*	sort using *k* kilobytes of memory
–z*n*	use *n* bytes of buffer for long lines
files	read standard input if *files* is – or no *files* are specified

+*pos1* [–*pos2*]

sort from *pos1* to *pos2*. If *pos2* is not specified, sort from *pos1* to end of line. The format for *pos1* and *pos2* is:

m[.*n*] [**bdfinr**]

m	*m* fields from start of line (default **0**)
n	*n* characters from start of field (default **0**)
bdfinr	option applies to specified key only

Examples:

Sort **file** using third character of second field as the sort key

$ sort +1.2f –1.3f file

Sort password file on group field using : as the field separator

$ sort –t":" –u +3n –4 /etc/passwd

spell - Find Spelling Errors (MISC)

$ spell [*options*] [*files*]

Description:

The **spell** command checks the words from *files* for spelling.

Options:

–b	check British spelling
–l	follow chains of included files
–v	display derivations and words not in the spelling list

–x	display possible stems with = for each word
+*wfile*	remove words contained in *wfile* from output
files	read standard input if no *files* are specified

Examples:

Check the spelling in **let.txt**

```
$ spell –v let.txt
```

spellin - Create Spelling List from Hash Codes (**MISC**)

$ /usr/lib/spell/spellin *n*

Description:

The **spellin** command reads *n* hash codes from standard input and displays a compressed spelling list on standard output.

split - Break File into Smaller Files (**FILE**)

$ split [–*n*] [*file*[*name*]]

Description:

The **split** command splits *file* into a set of *n*-line files.

Options:

–*n*	split *file* into *n*-line pieces (default **1000**)
file	read standard input if *file* is – or no *file* is specified
name	send output to *name***aa**, *name***ab**, **. . .** *name***zz** (default *name* is **xaa**)

Examples:

Split **file** into 100-line files, using **out** as the output prefix

```
$ split –100 file out
```

srchtxt – Search Message Data Base (**MISC**)

$ srchtxt [*options*] [*text*]

Description:

The **srchtxt** command displays parts of all of a message data base according to the given options.

Options:

–l *locale*	access files in **/usr/lib/locale/***locale***/LC_MESSAGES**
–m *file*	access given message file. Multiple messages files must be separated with a comma. If *file* begins with **/**, then it is interpreted as a pathname, otherwise **/usr/lib/locale/***locale***/LC_MESSAGES** searched
–s	suppress printing of message numbers
text	search for string or regular expression *text*

Variables:

LC_MESAGES
contains name of message file directory (default **/usr/lib/locale/C/LC_MESSAGES**)

Examples:

Display all message strings for dutch locale

```
$ srchtxt –l dutch
```

strings – Search Binary File for ASCII Strings (**MISC**)

$ strings [*options*] *files*

Description:

The **strings** command displays ASCII strings from binary *files*.

Options:

–o	precede each string by its octal offset in the file
–*n*	use *n* as minimum string length (default **4**)
–	search entire file for strings

Examples:

Check for strings in **hello**

$ strings hello | more

strip - Remove Symbol Table & Line Number Information (**MISC**)

$ strip [*options*] *files*

Description:

The **strip** command removes the symbol table and line number information from the specified object or archive files.

Options:

–l	strip line number information only
–V	display version information
–x	do not strip static or external symbol information

Examples:

Strip the line number information from all files in **/usr/lbin**

$ strip –l /usr/lbin/*

stty - Set Terminal Options (**MISC, BSD**)

$ stty [**–a**] [**–g**] [*options*]

$ /usr/ucb/stty [**–a**] [**–g**] [*options*]

Description:

The **stty** command sets terminal I/O options. If no options are given, display current settings. See local documentation for BSD options.

Options:

–a	display all options
–g	display settings in **stty** argument format

Control Modes:

[–]**clocal**	[enable] disable modem control
[–]**cread**	[disable] enable receiver
[–]**cstopb**	set [one] two stop bits per character
cs*n*	set character size to *n* bits (**5–8**)
[–]**hup**	same as **hupcl**
[–]**hupcl**	[do not] hang up on last close
ispeed *n*	set input baud rate to *n*
[–]**loblk**	[do not] block output from a non-current layer
ospeed *n*	set output baud rate to *n*
[–]**parenb**	[disable] enable parity generation and detection

[–]parext	[disable] enable detection of mark and space parity
[–]parodd	select [even] odd parity
0	hang up line immediately
n	set baud rate to**110**, **300**, **600**, **1200**, **1800**, **2400**, **4800**, **9600**, **19200**, **38400**

Input Modes:

[–]brkint	[do not] signal INTR on break
[–]icrnl	[do not] map carriage returns to newlines
[–]ignbrk	[do not] ignore break
[–]igncr	[do not] ignore carriage returns
[–]ignpar	[do not] ignore parity errors
[–]imaxbel	[do not] echo bell when input line is too long
[–]inlcr	[do not] map newlines to carriage returns
[–]inpck	[disable] enable parity checking
[–]istrip	[do not] strip characters to seven bits
[–]iuclc	[do not] map upper case to lower case
[–]ixany	allow [XON] any character to restart output
[–]ixoff	[disable] enable XON/XOFF input control
[–]ixon	[disable] enable XON/XOFF output control
[–]parmrk	[do not] mark parity errors

Output Modes:

bs*n*	set backspace delay to *n* (**0–1**)
cr*n*	set carriage return delay to *n* (**0–3**)
ff*n*	set form-feed delay to *n* (**0–1**)
nl*n*	set newline delay to *n* (**0–10**)
[–]ocrnl	[do not] map carriage returns to newlines
[–]ofdel	set fill characters to [NULL] DEL
[–]ofill	use [timing] fill characters for delay
[–]olcuc	[do not] map lower case to upper case
[–]onlcr	[do not] map newlines to carriage returns
[–]onlret	[no] carriage return after newline
[–]onocr	[do] do not output carriage return at column zero
[–]opost	[do not] post-process output
tab*n*	set output delay after *n* horizontal tabs (**0–3**)
vt*n*	set output delay after *n* vertical tabs (**0–1**)

Local Modes:

[–]echo	[do not] echo all input characters
[–]echoctl	[do not] echo control char's as ^*char*, delete a **^?**
[–]echoe	[do not] echo ERASE character
[–]echok	[do not] echo newline after KILL
[–]echoke	[does not] BS-SP-BS erase entire line on line kill
[–]echonl	[do not] echo newlines
[–]echoprt	[do not] echo erase character as character is "erased"
[–]flusho	[do not] flush output buffers
[–]icanon	[disable] enable ERASE and KILL processing
[–]iexten	[disable] enable extended functions for data input
[–]isig	[disable] enable INTR and QUIT checking
[–]lfkc	same as [**–echok**] **echok** (obsolete)

[–]noflsh [do not] flush after INTR and QUIT
[–]pendin [do not] retype pending input at next read
[–]stappl use [line] application mode on synchronous line
[–]stflush [disable] enable flush on synchronous line
[–]strap [enable] disable long line truncation on synchronous line
[–]stwrap [enable] disable line truncating on lines longer than 79 chars
[–]tostop [do not send] send SIGTOU on background process write
[–]xcase [unprocessed] processed upper/lower case

Hardware Flow Control Modes:

[–]cdxon [disable] enable CD hardware flow control on output
[–]ctsxon [disable] enableCTS hardware flow control on output
[–]dtrxoff [disable] enableDTR hardware flow control on input
[–]isxoff [disable] enable isochronous input hardware flow control
[–]rtsxoff [disable] RTS hardware flow control on input

Clock Modes:

rcibrg get receive clock from internal baud rate generator
rcrset get receive clock from receiver signal element timing lead, CCITT V.24 circuit 115, EIA-232-D pin 17
rctset get receive clock from transmitter signal element timing lead, CCITT V.24 circuit 114, EIA-232-D pin 15
rsetcoff receiver signal element timing clock not provided
rsetcrbrg output receive baud rate generator on receiver signal timing lead CCITT V.24 circuit 128, no EIA-232-D pin
rsetctbrg output transmit baud rate generator on receiver signal timing lead CCITT V.24 circuit 128, no EIA-232-D pin
rsetcrset output receiver signal element timing on receiver signal timing lead CCITT V.24 circuit 128, no EIA-232-D pin
rsetctset output transmitter signal element timing on receiver signal timing lead CCITT V.24 circuit 128, no EIA-232-D pin
tsetcoff transmitter signal element timing clock not provided
tsetcrbrg output transmit baud rate generator on transmitter signal timing lead CCITT V.24 circuit 113, EIA-232-D pin 24
tsetctset output receiver signal element timing on transmitter signal timing lead CCITT V.24 circuit 113, EIA-232-D pin 24
tsetctset output transmit signal element timing on transmitter signal timing lead CCITT V.24 circuit 113, EIA-232-D pin 24
xcibrg use internal baud rate generator for transmit clock
xcrset get transmit clock from receiver signal element timing lead, CCITT V.24 circuit 115, EIA-232-D pin 17
xctset get transmit clock from transmitter signal element timing lead, CCITT V.24 circuit 115, EIA-232-D pin 15

Control Assignments:

ctrl-char c set the control-character to *c*, where *ctrl-char* can be **ctab**, **discard**, **dsusp**,**eof**, **eol**, **eol2**, **erase**, **intr**, **kill**, **lnext**, **quit**, **reprint**, **start**, **stop**, **susp**, **swtch**, or **werase**
line *n* set the line discipline to *n* (**0–127**)
min *n* set **MIN** value to *c* (used with **–icanon**)
time *n* set **TIME** value to *c* (used with **–icanon**)

Combination Modes:

async	set normal asynchronous communications where clock settings are **xcibrg**, **rcibrg**, **tsetcoff**, **rsetcoff**
cooked	same as **–raw**
ek	set ERASE and KILL to **#** and @
[–]evenp	[disable] enable **parenb** and set **[cs8] cs7**
[–]lcase	[unset] set **xcase**, **iuclc**, **olcuc**
[–]LCASE	same as **[–]lcase**
–nl	set **icrnl**, **onlcr**; unset **inlcr**, **igncr**, **ocrnl**, **onlret**
nl	unset **icrnl**, **onlcr**; set **inlcr**, **igncr**, **ocrnl**, **onlret**
[–]parity	[disable] enable **parenb** and set **[cs8] cs7**
[–]oddp	[disable] enable **parenb**, **parodd** and set [cs8] cs7
[–]raw	[disable] enable raw input and output
sane	reset all modes to reasonable values
[–]tabs	[expand to spaces] preserve tabs
term	set modes for terminal; *term* can be **tek**, **ti700**, **tn300**, **tty33**, **tty37**, **vt05**

Window Size:

columns *n*	set window size to *n* columns
rows *n*	set windows size to *n* rows
xpixels *n*	set horizontal window size to *n* pixels
ypixels *n*	set vertical window size to *n* pixels

Examples:

\# Enable XON/XOFF; don't allow any char to restart output

$stty ixon –ixany

\# Set **erase** to <Backspace>

$ stty erase <Backspace>

su - Become Super-user or Another User (MISC)

$ su [–] [*name* [*args*]]

Description:

The **su** command is used to become a specified user or **root**. The invoker is prompted for a password (except for **root**). To restore the original environment, type **^D** or **exit**.

Options:

–	change to new users environment
args	specifies the arguments to pass to the new login shell

Files:

/etc/default/su

contains **su** configuration parameters:

CONSOLE	if defined, **su root** attempts are logged
PATH	if defined, contains default path
SULOG	if defined, contains name of **su** log file
SUPATH	if defined, contains default path for user invoking **su root**

/var/adm/sulog

contains records of **su** attempts

Examples:

\# Execute **chmod** as **root**

$ su –c "chmod 755 /tmp/ds.sh"

sum - Display File Checksum and Block Count (MISC, BSD)

$ sum [**–r**] *file*
$ /usr/ucb/sum *file*

Description:

The **sum** command displays the checksum & number of blocks for *file*.

Options:

–r	use an alternate checksum algorithm

sync - Update the Super Block (SYSTEM)

$ sync

Description:

The **sync** command updates the super block by flushing unwritten system buffers to disk. It executes the **sync** system call.

tabs - Set Terminal Tabs (MISC)

$ tabs [*options*] [**–T***type*] [**+m***n*]

Description:

The **tabs** command sets the tab stops for the invokers terminal according to the specified tab specifications.

Options:

Except for **–t** and **+m**, only one option can be given.

–a	Assembler, IBM S/370 format (1, 10, 16, 36, 72)
–a3	alternate Assembler, IBMS/370 format (1,10,16,40,72)
–c	normal COBOL format (1, 8, 12, 16, 20, 55)
–c2	compact COBOL format (1, 6, 10, 14, 49)
–c3	alternate compact COBOL format (1, 6, 10, 14, 18, 22, 26, 30, 34, 38, 42, 46, 50, 54, 58, 62, 67)
–f	FORTRAN format (1, 7, 11, 15, 19, 23)
–p	PL/1 format (1, 5, 9, 13, 17, 21, 25, 29, 33, 37, 41, 45, 53, 57, 61)
–s	SNOBOL format (1, 10, 55)
–T*term*	set the terminal type to *term* (default **$TERM**)
–u	UNIVAC Assembler format (1, 12, 20, 44)
+m *n*	move tabs *n* columns over (default **10**)
–*n*	set tabs at 1+*n* , 2+*n* , etc (default **8**)
n1,n2	arbitrary ascending values
– –*file*	read tab specifications from first line of *file*

Examples:

Set the tab stops at columns **7**, **14**, **21**, **28**, and **70**
$ tabs 7,14,21,28,70

tail - Display Last Part of a File (FILE, BSD)

$ tail [*options*] [*file*]
$ /usr/ucb/tail [*options*] [*file*]

Description:

The **tail** command displays a file starting at a specified place relative to the beginning or end of *file*. If no *options* are specified, display last ten lines of *file*.

Options:

–f	don't quit at end of *file;* continue to display as it grows
–r	display in reverse order (**BSD**)
–n [**bcl**]	begin *n* units from end of *file* (default **10l**)
+*n* [**bcl**]	begin *n* units from beginning of *file* (default **10l**)
bcl	units may be **b** blocks, **c** characters, or **l** lines
file	read standard input if no *file* is specified

Examples:

\# Display **file** as it is being written to

$ tail –f file

\# Start displaying **log** at line 20

$ tail +19 log

talk - Write to Another User (MISC, BSD)

$ talk *user* [*tty*]

$ /usr/ucb/talk *user* [*tty*]

Description:

The **talk** command copies lines from the invoker's to the *users* terminal. The terminal name can be given if *user* is logged in on more than one terminal. Permission to talk is controlled by **mesg**.

Options:

user	given as *host!user*, *host.user*, *host:user* or *user@host*
tty	specify *tty* if user logged in more than once

Examples:

\# Talk to **smith** logged onto **/dev/tty14**

$ talk smith tty14

tar - Tape File Archiver (FILE)

$ tar [*options*] [*modifiers*] [*directories*]

$ tar [*options*] [*modifiers*] [*files*]

Description:

The **tar** command copies files to and from directories or files. One option, followed by one or more modifiers can be given.

Options:

–c	create a new tape (implies **–r**)
–r	append *files* to the end of tape
–t	display the names of files on the tape. If no *files* are specified, display the names of all files on the tape. Output format is similar to **ls –l**.
–u	update older files or add if not on the tape
–x	extract *files* from the tape; extract entire tape if no *files* given

Modifiers:

b *n*	set blocking factor to *n*. Blocking factor is automatically determined when using the **–x** or **–t** options. (default **20**)
f *device*	use *device* (default **/dev/mt/??**). If *device* is –, write to standard output or read from standard input.

l	display error messages if links cannot be resolved
L	follow symbolic links
m	do not restore modification times
o	set user and group id's to that of invoker (only with **–x**)
v	display each file name as processed
w	copy interactively; prompt for confirmation
ns	use tape drive *n* (**0–7**, default **0**) and speed *s* (**l**, **m**, or **h**, default **m**)

Examples:

Copy the contents of **dir** to a tape

$ tar –cf /dev/rmt1 dir

List the contents of a tar file **backup.tar**

$ tar –tvf backup.tar

Extract contents of tape; do not restore the modification times

$ tar –xf /dev/mt/1m

tee - Copy Standard Input to Standard Output and Files (**MISC**)

$ tee [**–a**] [**–i**] [*files*]

Description:

The **tee** command transcribes standard input to standard output and makes copies to the specified files.

Options:

–a	append output to *files* instead of overwriting
–i	ignore interrupts

Examples:

Mail **uustat** output to admin and save a copy in **uustat.out**

$ uustat –q | tee uustat.out | mail admin

telnet - Communicate Using TELNET Protocol (**MISC**)

$ telnet [*system* [*port*]]

Description:

The **telnet** command communicates with *system* using TELNET protocol. If no *system* is given, command mode is entered.

Commands:

close close any open TELNET sessions and exit

display [*args*]
display specified **set** and **toggle** args (default all)

mode *type* set specified mode (**character** or **line**)

open *host* [*port*]
open a connection to *host* on default or given port

quit same as **close**

send *args* send special character sequences to remote host:

ao	abort output
ayt	are you there
brk	break
ec	erase character
el	erase line

	escape	escape
	ga	go ahead
	ip	interrupt process
	nop	no operation
	synch	SYNCH (discard unread input)
	?	display help menu for **send**
set *var value*		
	set **telnet** *variable* to *value*	
	echo	toggle local echo (default **^E**)
	eof	end of file character for remote
	erase	erase character
	escape	escape character
	flushoutput	abort output
	interrupt	interrupt process
	kill	erase line
	quit	break
status	display status	
toggle *flags*	toggle given flags:	
	autoflush	suspend display on **ao**, **intr**, or **quit** until ack received from remote
	autosynch	synch after **intr** or **quit** (default off)
	crmod	map <CR> to <CR<LF> (no default)
	debug	toggle socket level debugging(default off)
	localchars	recognize **flush**, **interrupt**, **quit**, **erase**, &
	kill	characters locally and transform to remote control sequences (default on in line mode, off in character mode)
	netdata	toggle hex display of data(default off)
	options	toggle display of internal protocol processing
	?	display local **toggle** commands
z	suspend **telnet**	
? [*cmd*]	display help for all or the specified command	

test - Evaluate Expression (MISC, BSD)

$ test *expression*

$ [*expression* **]**

$ /usr/ucb/test *expression*

Description:

The **test** command evaluates the specified expression and returns a zero (if true) or non-zero (if false) exit status. Arguments (brackets, flags, and operators) should be separated with spaces. Valid BSD expressions are [**d f n p r s t w z eq ge gt le lt ne**].

Expressions:

–b *file*	true if *file* exists and is a block special file
–c *file*	true if *file* exists and is a character special file
–d *file*	true if *file* exists and is a directory
–f *file*	true if *file* exists and is a regular file
–g *file*	true if *file* exists and its set-group-ID bit is set
–k *file*	true if *file* exists and its sticky bit is set
–L *file*	true if *file* exists and is a symbolic link
–n *string*	true if length of *string* is not zero

–p *file*	true is *file* exists and is a named pipe
–r *file*	true if *file* exists and is readable
–s *file*	true if *file* exists and its size is greater than zero
–t *n*	true if file descriptor *n* is open and associated with a terminal device
–u *file*	true if *file* exists and its set-user-ID bit is set
–w *file*	true if *file* exists and is writable
–x *file*	true if *file* exists and is executable
–z *string*	true if the length of *string* is zero
n1 **–eq** *n2*	truc if integers *n1* and *n2* are equal
n1 **–ge** *n2*	true if integers *n1* >= *n2*
n1 **–gt** *n2*	true if integers *n1* > *n2*
n1 **–le** *n2*	true if integers *n1* <= *n2*
n1 **–lt** *n2*	true if integers *n1* < *n2*
n1 **–ne** *n2*	true if integers *n1* and *n2* are not equal
string	true if *string* is not null
str1= *str2*	true if *str1* is equal to *str2*
str1!=*str2*	true if *str1* is not equal to *str2*

Operators:

!*expression*	not *expression*
exp1 **–a** *exp2*	*exp1* and *exp2*
exp1 **–o** *exp2*	*exp1* or *exp2*
\(*expr* \)	parentheses for grouping

Examples:

Display message if a file is not a directory and is writable

$ test \(! –d file –a –w file \) && echo "file writable"

tftp - Trivial File Transfer Protocol (MISC, BSD)

$ tftp [*host*]

$ /usr/ucb/tftp [*host*]

Description:

The **tftp** command transfers files to *host*.

Commands:

ascii	set transfer mode to ascii (default)
binary	set transfer mode to binary
connect host [*port*]	set host and optional port for transfers
get *files*	copy *files* from remote host; *files* can be given as *host:file* if remote hot not previously specified
mode [*mode*]	set file transfer mode to *mode* (**ascii** or **binary**)
put *files*	copy *files* to remote host; *files* can be given as *host:file* if remote hot not previously specified
quit	exit from **tftp**
rexmt *n*	set per packet retransmission timeout to *n* seconds
status	display current status
timeout *n*	set total transmission timeout to *n* seconds
trace	toggle packet tracing
verbose	toggle verbose mode
?	display help information

time - Time a Command (**MISC**)

$ time *command*

Description:

The **time** command diplays the elapsed time, system time, and execution time spent executing *command*.

Examples:

Time the **txfer** command

$ time txfer

timex - Time a Command and Display System Activity (**SYSTEM**)

$ timex [*options*] *command*

Description:

The **timex** command displays the elapsed time, system time, and execution time spent executing *command*. Process accounting information for the command and its children is also displayed.

Options:

–o	display total number of blocks read or written and total characters transferred
–p	display the process accounting records for *command*. Suboptions modify the data items reported:
–f	display fork/exec flag and system exit status
–h	display fraction of total CPU time used
–k	display total kcore-minutes
–m	display mean core size
–r	display CPU factor (user/(system+ user) times)
–t	display separate system and user CPU times
–s	display all activity for execution interval (see **sar**)

Examples:

Display execution time and CPU factor for **rcp**

$ timex rcp –r *.c mhost:/tmp

touch - Update Access/Modification Times of Files (**FILE, BSD**)

$ touch [**–amc**] [*time*] *files*

$ /usr/ucb/touch [**–cf**] [*time*] *files*

Description:

The **touch** command updates the access and modification times for *files*. Files are created if they do not exist.

Options:

–a	update access times only (default)
–m	update modification times only (default)
–c	do not create *file* if non-existent
–f	force touch regardless of read/write permissions
time	format is *mmddhhmm[yy]* (default current time)

Examples:

Set the access and modification time of **file** to **1231235892**

$ touch 1231235892 file

tput - Manipulate Terminal Attributes (**MISC**)

$ tput [**–T***term*] *attribute* [*parameters*]

$ tput –S <<

Description:

The **tput** command displays or sets terminal attributes.

Options:

–S <<*c*	set multiple attributes; each attribute must be on a line by itself, and input is terminated with char *c* on line by itself
–T*term*	query the database for terminal type *term*
attribute	specifies an attribute from the **terminfo** database

Comon Attributes:

bold	enable bold mode
clear	clear screen and move cursor to home
cols	display number of columns on screen
cup *x y*	move cursor to row *x* column *y*
home	move cursor home
init	display terminal initialization string
lines	display number of lines on screen
longname	display long terminal name
reset	display terminal reset string
rev	enable reverse video
rmso	disable standout mode
rmul	disable underscore mode
smso	enable standard out
smul	enable underscore mode

Variables:

TERM	contains name of terminal type

Examples:

Set the terminal type to **term**

$ tput –Tterm reset

Display the number of columns for the current terminal

$ tput cols

Enable reverse video mode

$ tput rev

tr - Translate Characters (**MISC, BSD**)

$ tr [**–cds**] [*string1*] [*string2*]

$ /usr/ucb/tr [**–cds**] [*string1*] [*string2*]

Description:

The **tr** command copies standard input to standard output and translates characters from *string1* into characters in *string2*. The \ character can be used to remove special meaning of characters or specify an octal digit *n* for an ASCII code.

Options:

–c	complement *string1* with octal **001–377**
–d	delete characters in *string1* from input
–s	truncate repeated characters from *string2*

Strings:

[**a–z**]	specifies a range of characters from **a** to **z**
[**c***n*]	specifies *n* repetitions of **c**. If the first digit in *n* is **0**, *n* is interpreted as octal. (default decimal)

Examples:

Translate upper case letters in **file** to lower case

$ cat file | tr '[a–z]' '[A–Z]'

Truncate double-spaced lines to one line

$ tr –s "\012" < file

true - Return Successful Exit Status (**MISC**)

$ true

Description:

The **true** command returns a successful (or zero) exit status.

Examples:

Execute **date** forever

$ while true; do date; done

truss – Trace Systems Calls and Signals (**PROG**)

$ truss [*options*] *command*

 # truss –p [*options*] *process-id*

Description:

The **truss** command executes *command* and produces a trace of its system calls, signals, and machine faults. A currently running process can also be traced with the **–p** option.

Options:

For options that take arguments, **all** can be given to specify all arguments, and **!** can be given to negate an argument. Multiple option arguments must be separated with a comma.

–a	display arguments passed in each **exec()**
–c	display count of system calls,faults and signals
–e	display environment strings passed in each **exec()**
–f	follow all children created by **fork()**
–i	do not display interruptable sleeping system calls
–m[!]*fault*	specify machine faults to trace or exclude (default **–mall –m!fltpage**)
–o *file*	send output to *file* (default **stderr**)
–p	trace *process-id* (only by super-user, or if invoker has same user id and group id as process)
–r[!]*fd*	display buffer contents for reads on given file descriptor *fd* (default **–r!all**)

–s[!]*sig*	specify signals to trace or exclude (default **–sall**)
–t[!]*call*	specify system calls to trace or exclude (default **–tall**)
–v[!]*call*	display structure contents passed by address to the specified system calls (default **–v!all**)
–w[!]*fd*	display buffer contents for each **write**() on any of the given file descriptors (default **–w!all**)
–x[!]*call*	display call arguments in raw format (default **–x!all**)

Examples:

\# Trace only **open()** and **close()** system calls for **xlog**

$ truss –t open,close xlog

\# Display count of system calls, signals & faults for process **1723**

$ truss –c –p 1723

tset/reset - Set Terminal Characteristics (BSD)

$ /usr/ucb/tset [*options*]

$ /usr/ucbreset [*options*]

Description:

The **tset** command initializes terminal characteristics. The **reset** command sets **cooked** and **echo** modes, disables **cbreak** and **raw** modes, enables newline translation, and restores special characters to a normal state before initializing.

Options:

–e*c*	set the erase character to *c* (default <backspace>)
–i*c*	set the interrupt character to *c* (default **^C**)
–l	do not display printing terminal initialization strings
–k*c*	set the line kill character to *c* (default **^X**)
–m*type*	specify terminal type for generic port connection
–n	specify new tty driver mode initialization
–Q	do not display **erase** and **kill** setting messages
–s	display **csh** initialization for **TERM**, and **TERMCAP**
–	display the terminal type

tsort - Sort Items (MISC)

$ tsort [*file*]

Description:

The **tsort** command produces an ordered list of items in *file* or standard input if no *file* is specified.

tty - Display Terminal Name (MISC)

$ tty [**–l**] [**–s**]

Description:

The **tty** command displays the pathname of the invoker's terminal.

Options:

–l	display synchronous line number terminal is connected to
–s	do not display pathname; return exit code only

umask - Set File-Creation Mode Mask (**FILE**)

$ umask [*mode*]

Description:

The **umask** command sets the user file-creation mode mask to *mode*. If *mode* is not specified, the current user file-creation mode mask is displayed. The value of each digit is subtracted from the corresponding digit of the system file creation mode mask.

Options:

mode	three octal digits referring to read/write/execute permissions for owner, group amd other

Examples:

Set file-creation mask to remove write permission by others

$ umask 002

Set file-creation mask to remove write and execute permission

$ umask 033

uname - Display System Name and Other Attributes (**SYSTEM**)

$ uname [**–snrvma**]

 # uname [**–S** *sys*]

Description:

The **uname** command displays the name and other information about the current system. On some implementations, system name can be set by the super-user.

Options:

–a	display all information (same as **–m**, **–n**, **–r**, **–s**, **–v**)
–m	display machine hardware name
–n	display the nodename
–p	display host's processor type
–r	display the operating system release
–s	display the operating system name (default)
–S *system*	set the system name to *system* (super-user only; system dependent)
–v	display the operating system version

Examples:

Display the network nodename and processor type

$ uname –np

uncompress - Uncompress File (**FILE**)

$ uncompress [*options*] [*files*]

Description:

The **uncompress** command restores a file compressed with **compress**.

Options:

–c	write to standard output without modifying *files*

unget - Undo a Previous get of an SCCS File (SCCS)

$ unget [*options*] *files*

Description:

The **unget** command undoes a previous **get –e** on *files*. If *files* is a directory, all files in that directory beginning with **s.** are processed.

Options:

–n	do not remove the retrieved file
–r*delta*	remove the specified delta
–s	do not display the intended deltas SCCS ID
files	read file names from standard input if *files* is –

Examples:

\# Undo previous **get** on **s.file**; do not remove retrieved file

$ unget –n s.file

uniq - Report Duplicate Lines (FILE)

$ uniq [*options*[*file1*[*file2*]]

Description:

The **uniq** command removes duplicate adjacent lines from *file1* and places the output in *file2*.

Options:

–c	display a count of duplicate lines also
–d	display only duplicate lines once
–u	display only unique lines from the original file
–*n*	skip first *n* fields from start of line
+*n*	skip first *n* characters from start of field

Examples:

\# Display adjacent duplicate lines in **file**; ignore field 1

$ uniq –d –1 file

units - Convert Units (MISC)

$ units

Description:

The **units** command converts quantities in various scales into quantities in other scales. Most abbreviations, metric prefixes and units are recognized.

unpack - Expand Files (FILE)

$ unpack *file*

$ unpack *file***.z**

Description:

The **unpack** command expands the specified file that was created by **pack**. If *file* is given, **unpack** will search for *file***.z**. The expanded output is placed in *file*.

Examples:

\# Unpack **hello.c.z**

$ unpack hello.c.z

uptime, users, uucp

uptime - Display Length of Time System Has Been Up (**BSD**)

$ /usr/ucb/uptime

Description:

The **uptime** command displays the current time, the length of time system has been up, and average number of jobs in run queue over last 1, 5, and 15 minutes.

users - List Login Names of Current Users (**BSD**)

$ /usr/ucb/users

Description:

The **users** command displays login names of users currently logged on.

uucp - Copy Files to Another System (**MISC**)

$ uucp [*options*] *files dest*

Description:

The **uucp** command copies *files* to or from another system.

Options:

–c	use source file instead of copying to spooler (default)
–C	copy source file to the spooler before transmitting
–d	make necessary directories for file copy (default)
–f	do not make intermediate directories for file copy
–g*c*	use transmit grade *c* (see **uuglist** for available grades)
–j	display uucp job id
–m	send mail to requester when finished
–n*user*	notify *user* on remote system that file was sent
–r	queue request but do not start the transfer process
–s*path*	put transfer status in file specified by *path*
–x *n*	set debugging level to *n* (**0–9**); use a higher number for more debugging information

Source/Destination File Format:

system!*path*
system!*system*...!*path*

format for the source/destination files. If *path* is a directory, then the last part of source file is used. The *path* can be given as:

/path	full pathname
path	partial pathname becomes prefixed by current directory
~user	expanded to user's login directory
~/path	expanded to **/var/spool/uucppublic/***path*

Examples:

Copy **file** to the public directory for **user** on **sa2**

$ uucp file sa2!sa2!~user

Copy **file1** in **user**'s **PUBDIR** on **mhst** to **file** on local system

$ uucp mhst!/var/spool/uucppublic/file file

uudecode - Decode Binary File (FILE)

$ uudecode *file*

Description:

The **uudecode** command restores a binary file from the encoded *file*, along with the original mode and owner specified in the header. If no *file* given, decode standard input.

Examples:

Decode **file.dec**

 # uudecode file.dec

uuencode - Encode Binary File (FILE)

$ uuencode [*file*] *label*

Description:

The **uuencode** command encodes a binary *file*. The *label* argument specifies the output file name to use when decoding. If no *file* given, encode standard input.

Examples:

Encode binary file stats in stats.uuen

$ uuencode stats > stats.uuen

uuglist - Display Service Grade List (SYSTEM)

$ uuglist [*options*]

Description:

The **uuglist** command displays the list of service grades available on the system to use with the **–g** option with **uucp** and **uux**.

Options:

–u	display service grades available to users

Examples:

Display available service grades

$ uuglist –u

uulog - Display UUCP Log Information (MISC)

$ uulog [*options*]

Description:

The **uulog** command displays **uucp** or **uuxqt** log information for all or the specified system.

Options:

–f*system*	do "**tail –f**" on the file transfer log for *system*
–s*system*	display information about *system* (default all systems)
–x	check the **uuxqt** file for *system*
–*n*	display the last *n* lines of log information

Examples:

Display log information for **scal**

$ uulog –sscal

uuname, uupick, uustat

uuname - Display UUCP System Names (MISC)

$ uuname [*options*]

Description:

The **uuname** command displays names of systems known by **uucp**.

Options:

–c	display names of systems known by **cu**
–l	display local system name

Examples:

\# Display local system name

$ uuname –l

uupick - Process UUCP Files Interactively (MISC)

$ uupick [**–s** *system*]

Description:

The **uupick** command interactively processes **uucp** files sent to the invoker from all or the specified systems.

Options:

–s *system*	search **PUBDIR** for files from *system*

Commands:

a	move all files from *system* to the current directory
a *dir*	move all file from *system* to *dir*
d	delete file
m	move file to the current directory
m *dir*	move file to *dir*
p	display file contents
q, ^D	quit
!*cmd*	escape to the shell and execute the given command
<Return>	go on to the next file
*	display a command summary

uustat - Display UUCP Request Information (MISC)

$ uustat [**–a** | **–j** | **–k***id* | **–m** | **–n** | **–p** | **–q** | **–r***id*]

$ uustat [**–a**] [**–s***sys* [**–j**] [**–u***user*] [**–S***flags*]

$ uustat –t*system* [**–d***n*] [**–c**]

Description:

The **uustat** command displays the status of or cancels the specified uucp jobs. It can also display the status of connections.

Options:

–a	display all the current jobs in the queue
–c	display average queue time (default transfer time)
–d*n*	use *n* minutes for calculations (default **60**)
–j	list the total number of jobs displayed (with **–a** and **–s**)
–k*id*	remove job *id* from queue; only jobs owned by the invoker can be removed, unless invoker is super-user

–m	report accessibility of all machines
–n	suppress standard output, but no standard error
–p	execute **ps –flp** for process id's in the lock files
–q	display information about jobs queued for each system
–r*id*	reset modification time of job*id*
–s*system*	display status of all requests to *system*
–S*flags*	report job state; *flags* can be one or more:
	c completed jobs
	i interrupted jobs
	q queued jobs
	r running jobs
–t*system*	show average transfer rate or queue time for *system*
–u*user*	display status of requests for *user*

Examples:

Remove request **3891** from the queue

 # uustat –k3891

Display the status of requests for all systems

$ uustat –q

uuto - Public UNIX to UNIX File Copy (MISC)

$ uuto [*options*] *files destination*

Description: (see **uucp** for *files* and *destination* format)

The **uuto** command sends files to another system via **uucp**.

Options:

–m	send mail when the copy is complete
–p	copy files to the **uucp** spooler before transmission

Examples:

Send **file** to **fred** on **kahost** via **uucp**; send mail when finished

$ uuto –m file kahost!fred

uux - Execute Remove Unix Commands (MISC)

$ uux [*options*] [*system*!]*command*

Description:

The **uux** command is used to execute commands on remote systems. Input files can be specified from other systems, and the standard output can be redirected to other systems.

Options:

–a*name*	replace the invoker's id with *name* for notification
–b	return standard input to **uux** if exit status is non-zero
–c	use source file instead of copying to spooler (default)
–C	copy file to the spooler before processing
–g*c*	use transmit grade *c* (see **uuglist** for available grades)
–j	display uucp job id
–n*user*	notify *user* on remote system that file was sent
–p	same as **–**
–r	queue request but do not start the transfer process

–s*path*	put transfer status in file specified by *path*
–x *n*	set debugging level to *n* (**0–9**); use a higher number for more debugging information
–z	send the user notification if the execution is successful
–	use standard input for the command

Examples:

\# Print **file** on **hdsys**

$ pr file | uux –p hdsys!lp

vacation - Automatically Respond to Mail Messages (MISC, BSD)

$ vacation [*options*]

$ **/usr/ucb/vacation –I**

$ **/usr/ucb/vacation** *user*

Description:

The **vacation** command controls how mail messages are automatically saved and responded to. The reply for the BSD version taken from **~/.vacation.msg**. The **vacation** command should be specified in the **.forward** file.

Options:

–d	append date to the log file
–F *uid*	forward mail to *uid* if unable to save (default return to sender)
–F ""	disable automatic save and response
–I	initialize **~/.vacation.pag** and **~/.vacation.dir**. If **–I** not specified, read message from **stdin**. **(BSD)**
–l *file*	keep track of originators who have already received automatic response in *file* (default **$HOME/.maillog**)
–m *file*	save mail messages in *file* (default **$HOME/.mailfile**)
–M *file*	get message for automatic response from *file* (default **/usr/share/lib/mail/std_vac_msg**)

Examples:

\# Get automatic response from **$HOME/.automesg**

$ vacation –M $HOME/.automesg

\# Forward mail to **admin** if save problems encountered

$ vacation –F 105

val - Validate an SCCS File (SCCS)

$ val [**–s**] [**–r***SID*] [**–m***text*] [**–y***text*] *files*

$ val –

Description:

The **val** command checks the structure of the specified SCCS files. It returns an 8-bit code for the file status.

Options:

–m*text*	compare *text* with **%M%** keyword
–r*delta*	validate the specified delta
–s	do not display diagnostic messages
–y*text*	compare *text* with **%Y%** keyword
–	read command line arguments from standard input

Examples:

\# Validate delta **3.1** of **s.file**

$ val –r3.1 s.file

vc - Version Control (FILE)

$ vc [**–a**] [**–t**] [**–c***c*] [**–s**] [*keyword*=*value* **. . .**]

Description:

The **vc** command copies lines from standard input to standard output and replaces the specified keywords with their values. This command is obsolete and will be removed from the next release.

Options:

–a	replace keywords surrounded by control characters with their values in all text lines
–c*c*	use control character *c* (default "**:**")
–s	do not display warning messages
–t	ignore all characters from the beginning of the line up to and including the first tab character

vi/view/vedit - Edit Text (FILE)

$ vi [*options*] [*files*]
$ view [*options*] [*files*]
$ vedit [*options*] [*files*]

Description:

The **vi** command edits *files* according to *options*. The **view** command edits *files* with the **readonly** flag set. The **vedit** command edits *files* with **report** set to **1**, **novice** and **showmode** set, and **magic** set to **off**.

Options:

–c *cmd*	begin by executing the specified command
–C	edit an encrypted file; prompt for a key to use
–l	indent for lisp code
–L	list file names saved on editor or system crash
–r *file*	recover the last saved version of *file* (default list all files)
–R	set **readonly** mode (same as **view**)
–t *tag*	edit file with *tag* and position cursor at its definition
–w*n*	set default window size to *n* lines
–x	edit an encrypted file; prompt for a key to use for encrypting and decrypting text
+*cmd*	begin by executing the specified command

Modes:

The **vi** command operates in three modes:

command	normal and initial mode; other modes return to command mode on completion. Enter <Escape> to cancel partial commands.
input	entered with any of **a**, **A**, **c**, **C**, **i**, **I**, **o**, **O**, **R**, or **S**. Text can be entered after command. Enter <Escape> to terminate.
last line	reading input for **:**, **/**, **?**, or **!**. Enter <Return> to terminate.

File Manipulation Commands:

:args	display current argument list
:cd *dir*	change working directory of editor to *dir*
:e *file*	edit *file*
:e!	reedit current file; discard changes

:e +*n file*	edit *file* starting at line *n*
:e +*file*	edit *file* starting at last line
:e#	edit last file edited
:e! #	edit last file edited; discard changes
:f	display current file and line number
:n	edit next file in the argument list
:n *args*	specify a new argument list
:pre	preserve the buffer
:q	exit from the editor
:q!	exit from the editor; discard changes
:r *file*	insert *file* after the cursor
:r! *command*	read output of *command* into the buffer
:rec	retrieve buffer after a crash
:sh	escape to a subshell (**^D** to end)
:ta *tag*	edit file containing tag at *tag*
:ver	display editor version and release number
:*x,y* **w** [*file*]	write lines *x* through *y* to *file*
:*x,y* **w!** [*file*]	overwrite lines *x* through *y* to *file*
:w [*file*]	write to *file* (default use the current file)
:w! [*file*]	overwrite *file* (default use the current file)
ZZ	exit from the editor and save changes
:!*command*	execute *command* then return to the editor
:[*n***]!***command*	replace line *n* with output of *command*

Screen Positioning Commands:

[*n*]**^f**	move forward *n* screens
[*n*]**^b**	move backward *n* screens
[*n*]**^d**	move forward *n* lines
[*n*]**^u**	move backward *n* lines
[*n*]**^e**	move window down *n* lines
[*n*]**^y**	move window up *n* lines

Adjusting Screen:

^g	display status line on bottom line
^l	clear and redraw screen
^r	clear and redraw screen;
z<CR>	redraw screen; put cursor at top
z-<CR>	redraw screen; put cursor at bottom
z.<CR>	redraw screen; put cursor at middle
z*n* **.**<CR>	redraw screen; put cursor at line *n*
/*pat* **/ z–**<CR>	redraw screen; put cursor at *pat*
M	move to middle of screen
H	move to top of screen
L	move to bottom of screen

Line Positioning:

[*n*]**G**	move to line *n* (default last line)
n<CR>	move *n* lines forward
*n***k**	move backwards *n* lines
:*n*	move to line *n*
<CR>	move to start of next line
+	move to start of next line
–	move to start of previous line
j	move to next line, same column
^n	same as **j**
k	move to previous line, same column

Character/Word/Other Positioning:

[*n*]**h**	move left *n* characters
[*n*]**l**	move right *n* characters
[*n*]**j**	move down *n* characters
[*n*]**k**	move up *n* characters
[*n*]**w**	move forward *n* words
[*n*]**b**	move backwards *n* words
[*n*]**e**	move forward to end of *nth* word
[*n*]**W B E**	same as **w b e** but ignoring punctuation
[*n*])	move to *nth* next sentence
[*n*](	move to *nth* previous sentence
[*n*]}	move to *nth* next paragraph
[*n*]{	move to *nth* previous paragraph
[*n*]]]	move to *nth* next section
[*n*][[	move to *nth* previous section
%	find matching ( ), { }
^	move to first non-space character in line
$	move to end of current line
0	move to beginning of current line
[*n*] |	move to character position *n* (default **0**)
[*n*]<Space>	move right *n* characters
[*n*]<Backspace>	move left *n* characters

Pattern Searching:

/*pattern*<CR>	move forward to line matching *pattern*
?*pattern*<CR>	move backward to line matching *pattern*
/*pat*/±*n*<CR>	move forward to *nth* line after/before *pat*
?*pat*?±*n*<CR>	move back to *nth* line after/before *pat*
/<CR>	repeat last / search
?<CR>	repeat last **?** search
n	repeat last / or **?** search
N	repeat last / or **?** in opposite direction
f*c*	move forward to character *c* in current line
F*c*	move backward to character *c* in current line

t*c* — move forward to character before *c* in line

T*c* — move backward to character after *c* in line

; — repeat last **f F t T** command

, — same as **;** except in opposite direction

Search Patterns:

^ — beginning of line

$ — end of line

. — any one character

\ — take next character literally

* — any characters

[*string*] — any characters in *string*

[*a-z*] — any characters in range *a* to *z*

[^*string*] — any characters not in *string*

\< — beginning of word

\> — end of word

Inserting Text:

a — add after cursor

A — add to end of line

[*n*]**a***text*<Esc>
— add *n* copies of added *text*

[*n*]**A***text* <Esc>
— add *n* copies of added *text* to end of line

i — insert before cursor

I — insert before first non-blank in line

[*n*]**i***text* <Esc>
— insert *n* copies of inserted *text*

[*n*]**I***text* <Esc>
— insert *n* copies of inserted *text* before first non-blank in line

o — open line below cursor

O — open line above cursor

^h — erase last character inserted

^w — erase last word inserted

^d — backtab over autoindent

0^d — backtab over all autoindent in line

Corrections during Insert:

^H — delete last character inserted

^W — delete last word inserted

^D — backtab over autoindent

^^D — backtab to beginning of the line; do not reset left margin

0^D — backtab to beginning of the line; reset left margin

^V — quote non-printable character

**** — quote erase and kill characters

kill — remove current line of input

<Escape> — end insert mode; return to command mode

Operator Scope & Buffers:

Operator scope defines the limit of some commands, such as **c**hange, **d**elete, or **y**ank. The following lists operators and scope:

b	backwards to beginning of word
e	cursor to end of current word
w	cursor to beginning of next word
0	before cursor to end of current line
$	cursor to end of current line
(	before cursor back to beginning of sentence
)	cursor to end of sentence
{	before cursor back to beginning of paragraph
}	cursor to end of paragraph

Some commands, such as **put/Put**, or **Y**ank work with buffers. Buffers are addressed by preceding the buffer name with a dot. The following lists buffers and their descriptions:

1–9	buffers that hold last nine **y**ank or **d**elete operations
a–z	buffers that hold explicit **y**anks or **d**eletes
A–Z	same as **a–z**, except buffers are appended to
#	alternate buffer
%	current buffer

Deleting Text:

[*n*]**d***object*	delete *n* objects (see **Scope & Buffers**)
d$	delete to end of line
D	same as **d$**
[*n*]**dd**	delete *n* lines
"*n* **d**<CR>	delete to buffer *n* (see **Scope & Buffers**)
[*n*]**x**	delete *n* characters
[*n*]**X**	delete *n* characters to left of cursor

Changing/Replacing Text:

[*n*]**c***object*	change *n* objects (see **Scope & Buffers**)
[*n*]**C**	change *n* lines (default rest of line)
[*n*]**J**	join *n* lines
[*n*]**r**	replace character under cursor *n* times
[*n*]**R**	replace text from cursor to <Esc> *n* times
c$	change rest of line
s	substitute text from cursor to <Esc>
S,**cc**	substitute entire line
xp	reverse order of two characters
ddp	reverse order of two lines
:g/*s1***/***cmd*	execute *cmd* for lines matching *s1*
:v/*s1***/***cmd*	execute *cmd* for lines not matching *s1*

:g/*s1***/s//***s2***/***cmd*

change all occurrences of *s1* to *s2*

:s/*s1***/***s2***/***cmd*

change first *s1* to *s2* in line; *cmd* can be:

c	confirm each change
g	change every *s1* in current line
p	print changed lines

:*x,y* **[s,g,v]**...	limits range from lines *x* to *y* for **s**, **g**, or **v** operations
&	repeat last **:s** operation
~	change letters case
.	repeat last modification operation

Copying/Moving Text:

"[*buffer*][*n*]**Y**	copy *n* lines of text into *buffer* (default **1**)
[*n*]**Y**	copy *n* lines of text into default buffer
yy	same as **Y** command
[*n*]**y***operator*	copy *n* operators into default buffer
"[*buffer*][*n*]**y**	copy *n* operators into *buffer*
"[*buffer*]**p**	put contents of *buffer* after cursor
p	put contents of default buffer after cursor
"[*buffer*]**P**	put contents of *buffer* before cursor
P	put contents of default buffer before cursor
:*x,y* **t***n*	copy lines *x* to *y* after line *n*
:*x,y* **co***n*	same as **:***x,y***t***n*
:*x,y* **m***n*	move lines *x* to *y* after line *n*

Undo/Redo/Retrieve:

u	undo previous changes
U	restore current line
"*n***p**	retrieve *nth* last delete (from buffer *n*)
.	retrieve previous delete

Marking/Formatting:

m*x*	mark current position with character *x*
`*x*	move to mark *x*
'*x*	move to first character in line marked *x*
''	move to first character in line with previous mark
``	return to previous location after cursor motion
[*n*]**<<**	shift *n* lines left (see **sw** in Options)
[*n*]**>>**	shift *n* lines right (see **sw** in Options)
[*n*]**>***x*	indent *n* lines in *x* ((,), [[,]], {, }, **G**, **H**, **M**, **L**)
[*n*]**<***x*	remove indent from *n* lines in *x* (*x* can be (,), [[,]], {, }, **G**, **H**, **M**, **L**)

Macros:

:map *lhs rhs*	define character or escape sequence *lhs* to be equivalent to request combination *rhs*. Escape <CR>, <Esc>, newline, space or tab characters in *lhs* with **^v**.
:map ! *lhs rhs*	map applies to insert mode
:map	display maps on status line
:map!	display insert mode maps on status line
:unmap	*lhs* end map *lhs*
:unmap!	*lhs* end insert mode map

:abbr	display **abbr** abbreviations
:abbr *s1 s2*	substitute *s2* for *s1*
:una *s1*	delete *s1* abbreviation
@*macro*	invoke the specified macro
@@	repeat the last macro

Setting Options:

.exrc	set default options from **.exrc**
:set *option=value*	set *option* to *value*
:set *option*	set *option*
:set no*option*	unset *option*
:set all	display all option settings
:set *option?*	display *option* value on status line
EXINIT='*cmds*'	environment variable that also controls **vi** commands and options

Options:

[no]ai	[do not] set auto-indentation
ap	display current line after **cdJmstu**
[no]aw	[do not] set auto-write after **:n** and **!**
[no]bf	[do not] discard control characters from input (except formfeed, newline, tab)
directory=*dir*	use *dir* for temporary buffer file
[no]eb	[do not] suppress error bells
[no]edcompatible	[do not] make substitute work like in **ed**
ht=*n*	specify hardware tab settings to *n*
[no]ic	[do not] ignore upper/lower case for searches
nolisp	make (){}]][[LISP compatible
[no]list	[do not] show tabs as **^I**, end of line as **$**
[no]magic	[do not] make **.&^[*** special for searches
[no]mesg	[do not] allow messages from other users
[no]nu	[do not] provide line numbering
[no]opt	[do not] speed output; no auto<CR>
paragraphs=IPLPPPQPbpPLI	macro names that start paragraphs
[no]prompt	[do not] prompt for input with **:**
[no]ro	[do not] set file to **readonly**
[no]re	[do not] simulate smart terminal
report=*n*	set changed line status limit to *n*
scroll=*n*	set **z** scroll amount to *n* lines
sect=NNSHH HU	macro names that start sections
shell=*sh*	set pathname of shell to use
sw=*n*	set shift distance to *n* spaces
[no]showmode	[do not] display mode messages
[no]slow	[do not] delay display updates

[no]**sm**	[do not] show matching) } for ({
tl=*n*	set tab stops to *n* for **^i**
ts=*n*	set tab stops to *n*
term=*t*	set terminal to *t*
[no]**terse**	[do not] make error messages shorter
[no]**to**	[do not] set **map** time limit
ttytype=*t*	set ttytype to terminal type *t*
[no]**wa**	[do not] check write request
[no]**warn**	[do not] set **!** message to "**No write since last change**"
window=*n*	set number of lines in window to *n*
[no]**ws**	[do not] search wrap around boundaries
wrapmargin=*n*	start new line if *n* spaces from right

vmstat - Report Virtual Memory Statistics (BSD)

$ /usr/ucb/vmstat [*options*] [*drives*] [*m*] [*n*]

Description:

The **vmstat** command displays information about the cpu activity, disk, memory, processes, trap, and virtual memory.

Options:

–f	display number of **forks**, **vforks** and number of memory pages for each since startup
–i	display number of interrupts for each device since startup
–s	display page-related events total since startup
m	repeat statistics *m* times
drives	display information for *drives* only (default first four drives)
n	display information for last *n* seconds

w - Display Users Logged In and Current Activity (BSD)

$ /usr/ucb/w [*options*] [*user*]

Description:

The **w** command displays the current system activity.

Options:

–h	do not display the header
–l	display information in long format (default)
–s	display information in short format
user	display information about *user* only

wait - Wait for Completion of Process (SYSTEM)

$ wait [*n*]

Description:

The **wait** command waits for the specified background process to complete. If no process id given, wait for all background processes.

Examples:

Wait for process 7413 to complete

$ wait 7413

wall - Write to All Users (**MISC**)

$ wall

Description:

The **wall** command sends a message read from standard input to all currently logged-in users. End message with **^D**.

wc - Count Characters, Lines and Words (**MISC, BSD**)

$ wc [*options*] [*files*]
$ /usr/ucb/wc [*options*] [*files*]

Description:

The **wc** command counts the characters, lines, and/or words in *files*. If no options are given, display a count of all characters, lines, and words. A total count for all files is kept.

Options:

–c	display the number of characters (default all options)
–l	display the number of lines
–w	display the number of words
files	read standard input in no *files* are specified

Examples:

Display the number of **.c** files in the **SRC** directory
$ wc –l SRC/*.c

Display the numbers of characters and words in **file**
$ wc –cl file

what - Identify SCCS Files (**SCCS**)

$ what [**–s**] *files*

Description:

The **what** command searches *files* for the pattern beginning with **@#** and ending with a **"**, **>**, newline, ****, or the null character and displays it. The pattern is what **get** uses to replace the **%Z%** keyword.

Options:

–s	return the first occurrence of the **%Z%** keyword only

Examples:

Display the version of **hello.**
$ what hello

whatis - Describe What a Command Is (**BSD**)

$ /usr/ucb/whatis *command*

Description:

The **whatis** command displays the header line from the manual section for the specified command.

whereis - Locate Source, Binary and/or Manual for Files (**BSD**)

$ **/usr/ucb/whereis** [*options*] *files*

Description:

The **whereis** command locates the source, binary, and/or manual section for the specified files.

Options:

–b	search for binaries only
–B *dirs*	search for binaries in *dirs* only
–f	used to separate **–B** *dirs* and *file* args
–m	search for manual sections only
–M *dirs*	search for manual sections in *dirs* only
–s	search for source only
–S *dirs*	search for source in *dirs* only
–u	look for *files* with missing source, binary, manual sections

who - Display Who is Logged On (**SYSTEM**)

$ who [–abdHlqprstTu] [*file*]

$ who –qn *x* [*file*]

$ who am i

$ who am I

Description:

The **who** command displays who is currently logged on system along with terminal line, login time, process id of shell, and elapsed time since activity has occurred. Other information, such as last reboot time, system time change, and logoffs can also be displayed.

Options

–a	process **/var/adm/utmp** or *file* with all options
–b	display time and date of last reboot
–d	display finished processes not respawned by **init**
–H	display column headings
–l	list lines open for **login**; list name field as **LOGIN**
–n *n*	display *n* users per line (default **1**)
–q	display names and number of users only
–p	display active processes spawned by **init**
–r	display current run-level of **init**
–s	display names, terminal lines login times only (default)
–t	display last change to system clock
–T	display currently logged in users, terminal line, login time, and tty state. Display **+** if terminal is writable, – if not writable, or **?** if the line is bad.
–u	display currently logged in users. Display **.** if terminal has been active in last minute and **old** if it has been inactive for more than 24 hours since last boot.
am i	identify invoking user
am I	same as **who am i**
file	get login information from *file* (default **/var/adm/tmp**)

Examples:

\# Check if **user** is logged in

$ who –u | grep user

\# Display the current run level

$ who –r

\# Display time of last reboot

$ who –b

whoami - Display Effective Current User Id (**BSD**)

$ /usr/ucb/whoami

Description:

The **whoami** command displays the effective user id.

whois – Internet Name Directory Service (**MISC, BSD**)

$ whois [**–h** *host*] *name*

$ /usr/ucb/whois *name*

Description:

The **whois** command checks for an Internet directory entry that matches name.

Options:

–h *host*	search on *host*
name	user name or handle; *name* can also be given as:
	!*name* — match handle only
	.*name* — match name only
	name... — match anything beginning with name
	**name* — match group or organization name

Examples:

\# Look up entry for **Jill Bailey**

$ whois .Bailey Jill

\# Look up entry for organization **ARC**

$ whois !ARC

\# Look up entry that matches handle starting with **Com**

$ whois Com...

write - Write to Another User (**MISC**)

$ write *user* [*tty*]

Description:

The **write** command copies what is typed into the invoker's terminal to another user's terminal. The recipient is prompted, unless **mesg** is set to **n**. If recipient is logged in more than once, the *tty* can be given to specify which line to write to. If first character of a line begins with **!**, the rest of the line in executed by the shell.

xargs, xstr, yacc, zcat

xargs - Construct Argument List and Execute Command (MISC)

$ xargs [*options*] [*command* [*arguments*]]

Description:

The **xargs** command combines *arguments* with arguments read from standard input and executes the given command one or more times.

Options:

–e*string*	set EOF to *string* (default _)
–i*string*	use *string* as argument to *command*
–l*n*	execute *command* for each *n* lines of *arguments*
–n*n*	execute *command* with a maximum of *n* arguments
–p	prompt the user for each command invocation
–s*n*	set max size of argument list to *n* characters (default **470**)
–t	echo *command* and argument list
–x	exit if argument list is greater than *n* characters from **–s**

Examples:

Prompt to remove files in the current directory

$ ls | xargs –p –l rm –rf

xstr - Extract Strings from C Programs (BSD)

$ /usr/ucb/xstr [*options*] [*file*.**c**]

Description:

The **xstr** command extracts strings from the C source file. The new C source version is placed in **x.c**,and the strings are placed in **xs.c**.

Options:

– c	extract strings from *file*.**c**
file.**c**	read **stdin** if *file*.**c** is **–**

yacc - Yet Another Compiler Compiler (PROG)

$ yacc [*options*] *file*

Description:

The **yacc** command converts a context-free grammar into a set of tables for an LR(1) parsing algorithm.

Options:

–d	put **#define** statements in **y.tab.h**
–l	do not put **#line** constructs in **y.tab.c**
–Qn	suppress tool id information (default)
–Qy	include tool id information in output
–t	compile debugging code
–v	put parse tables and grammer reports in **y.output**
–V	display version information

zcat - Show Compressed Files (FILE)

$ zcat [*file*.**Z**]

Description:

The **zcat** command displays the specified compressed files.

DOWNLOADABLE SCRIPTS AND TIPS

Selected examples of code from ASP publications are available for free downloading from the ASP website. Now you can study and customize these programs without tedious keyboarding.

To take advantage of this special ASP customer service, visit our website at <**www.aspinc.com**>. From our Download Requests page you may choose examples from a variety of ASP publications.

QUICK REFERENCE PUBLICATIONS FROM ASP

Bourne Shell Quick Reference Guide

The Bourne Shell was the original shell for UNIX, and it still remains the most widely used and distributed. The ***Bourne Shell Quick Reference Guide*** summarizes this scripting language and includes complete sample programs and examples. Many UNIX commands used in Bourne Shell scripting are also included.

C Shell Quick Reference Guide

The C Shell was developed as a replacement for the standard Bourne shell and is found on most systems running UNIX. The ***C Shell Quick Reference Guide*** covers this scripting language and includes complete sample programs and examples. Many UNIX commands used in C Shell scripting are also included.

Korn Shell Quick Reference Guide

The Korn Shell is an interactive command and programming language that provides an interface to UNIX and other systems. The ***Korn Shell Quick Reference Guide*** covers all aspects of the Korn Shell, with complete Korn shell scripts and many examples included.

JavaScript Quick Reference Guide

JavaScript is a cross-platform, object-based scripting language for client and server applications. The ***JavaScript Quick Reference Guide*** covers this scripting language and includes complete sample programs and practical examples.

Quick Reference Cards

Vi, C, C++, SCCS, HTML Reference Cards

Multi-fold cards provide concise summaries for programmers and users.

For order information, email books@aspinc.com